THE TRANSITION COACH

A DENTIST'S GUIDE TO FINANCIAL INDEPENDENCE

BY BARRY R. MCNULTY

TRAFFORD

Note for Librarians: a cataloguing record for this book that includes Dewey Decimal Classification and US Library of Congress numbers is available from the National Library of Canada. The complete cataloguing record can be obtained from the National Library's online database at:
www.nlc-bnc.ca/amicus/index-e.html
ISBN 1-4120-3563-5

TRAFFORD

Offices in Canada, USA, Ireland, UK and Spain
This book was published on-demand in cooperation with Trafford Publishing. On-demand publishing is a unique process and service of making a book available for retail sale to the public taking advantage of on-demand manufacturing and Internet marketing. On-demand publishing includes promotions, retail sales, manufacturing, order fulfilment, accounting and collecting royalties on behalf of the author.
Book sales in Europe:
Trafford Publishing (UK) Ltd., Enterprise House, Wistaston Road Business Centre, Wistaston Road, Crewe, Cheshire CW2 7RP UNITED KINGDOM
phone 01270 251 396 (local rate 0845 230 9601)
facsimile 01270 254 983; orders.uk@trafford.com
Book sales for North America and international:
Trafford Publishing, 6E–2333 Government St., Victoria, BC V8T 4P4 CANADA
phone 250 383 6864 (toll-free 1 888 232 4444)
fax 250 383 6804; email to orders@trafford.com

www.trafford.com/robots/04-1391.html

10 9 8 7 6 5 4 3 2

"Barry is very thorough in his research and analysis and he explains everything in layman's terms so that we understand and are comfortable with our decisions. He has a conservative approach (in keeping with our philosophy), but the return on our investments is ahead of the markets and we are on track to be in a position to retire when we planned, if that's our choice."

Dr. Ron McWade

"Over the past 10 years, Barry McNulty has helped us to establish a better vision of our future and to develop an incremental, step by step program to achieve our goal. We know that the transition from dentistry will be more focused on the emotional aspects of the time rather than the financial concerns."

Dr. Ken Southward

"Several years ago I enlisted the services of Barry McNulty based on reading many excellent articles written by Barry and by hearing him speak. I was impressed by his boundless knowledge of things financial as it pertained to me and my dental practice. His great sense of humour and from the heart approach also appealed to me immediately."

Dr. Paul Goodman

"Thanks to Barry McNulty's timely advice, the crash of 2000 did not negatively impact my portfolio, enabling me to retire as originally planned."

Dr. Peter Kalman

"Barry McNulty has literally 'got it all together'. He has an in-depth knowledge and appreciation of professional practitioners and how their financial planning requires a combination of the personal and professional aspects of their lives."

Dr. Bernie Dolansky

CONTENTS

INTRODUCTION

In the course of your lifetime you'll go through many types of transitions. They're a fact of life. Some of them can be delayed, but most of them can't be avoided. Some happen naturally, such as the progression from childhood to adolescence to adulthood. Others require decision-making and appropriate follow through. When it comes to your dental practice, taking the time and necessary steps to plan for your transition is vitally important. It's not something to leave to chance.

Think of it this way. Imagine taking a long drive to a remote location that you've never been to before. Would you load the family into the car one beautiful morning and start out without any preparation? Not likely. Nor would you want to leave without being sure of such vital facts as the condition of your car or being able to get sufficient fuel and food along the way. When it comes to making this type of journey being properly prepared makes sense, doesn't it?

Here's the point. We're all familiar with driving a car on a long journey and this is what makes it easy to see the importance of preparation and planning. This isn't the case with transition planning. It's not something that you do regularly. In fact, throughout your lifetime you may do a transition of this type only once. But that doesn't eliminate the need for appropriate preparation – it actually makes it more important.

In fact, dealing with your transition is a lot more complex than planning a car trip. There aren't many comprehensive road maps immediately available to guide you on your dental transition journey.

So how do you go about it?

What are the right questions to ask?

What are the concerns and pitfalls you should watch for?

Helping you find answers to those questions and others is why I wrote this book. I want to provide you with a road map to help you in a proactive manner plan the transition that's right for you.

Over the course of your transition you'll likely be working with, at one stage or another, your accountant, insurance representative, lawyer, investment advisor, banker, practice valuator, practice broker, and other professionals. You can't do everything yourself, so think of them as your transition team. To function properly, every team needs a coach to coordinate their efforts and focus on common goals and objectives. This is the person who organizes everyone's special abilities and talents into a cohesive group. This book will help you fulfill the important role of coach, as it relates to your team and your ideal transition. You may choose to act as coach yourself or you may wish to delegate the responsibility to one of your trusted advisors. But keep in mind that delegating doesn't mean abdicating!

Regardless of the approach you take, this book will facilitate your understanding of the transition process. You'll know what questions to ask, what concerns should be addressed, and how to recognize existing opportunities that will give you greater control over the process. In short, this book is intended to put you in the coach's box so that you can personally plan your own transition.

Finances play a key role in transition

Everyone's transition preferences are individual, but for most people financial considerations influence decision-making. After all, money is more than just a medium of exchange in our society. Human beings tend to be concerned with "status", and money (or the lack of it) has a strong influence on one's place in society. If you're financially successful, your friends, colleagues, neighbours, and family are more likely to admire and respect you.

Financial success even has a strong influence on how you view yourself. Without sufficient money you may not have the freedom to live your life to what you might describe as the "fullest". Financial stress is difficult to bear. It can affect your health, your relationships, and even your ability to provide security for yourself and your family from life's random challenges. Of course it's important to keep in mind that money is relative.

What's sufficient for you may not be for another person.

It's also important to remember that transitions come in many forms with multiple variations. Some people plan on selling their practice and retiring to their idea of the good life, without ever looking back. Others prefer the idea of a staged transition where they sell part of their practice, allowing them to slow down but at the same time continue to enjoy the benefits of ownership. Still others choose to sell out, but do so with the proviso that they can continue to associate for a specified period of time. Six months or one year is common when the purpose is to facilitate the transfer of patient goodwill to the buyer, but other associate arrangements may involve a much longer period of time.

CASE STUDY

Dr. B practiced dentistry in a bedroom community about an hour's drive from a major urban centre. He was in his early fifties, married and had four children, ranging from 7 to 16 years of age. He had a profitable practice and was in good shape financially. While he didn't want to stop practicing entirely, he saw merit in cutting back to three days a week. But his problem was one of growth.

The area where he was located had expanded dramatically and so had Dr. B's practice. He had tried working with a couple of associates, but it hadn't worked out. The office, located in a small house he purchased 20 years ago, was getting cramped and they were out of room. Renovating or even moving would be an expensive undertaking. Given the uncertain outlook for the future of practice values, Dr. B was rightly concerned that he may not be able to recoup his investment for an expansion or renovation by the time he wanted to retire.

One alternative would have been to simply reduce his hours and stop taking new patients. But this would create a negative impact on the value of the practice he'd worked so hard to build over the years. He was proud of his accomplishments at the office, and letting the goodwill value deteriorate didn't feel right to him. Thankfully, Dr. B's story has a happy ending. He decided to sell the practice, and in the transition, the purchaser was more than happy to agree to keep Dr. B on as an associate.

Six Step Transition Planning Process

No matter what kind of transition you decide on, the Six Step Transition Planning Process outlined in this book provides you with a dependable roadmap for your journey. Here's a top line look at that process ...

Step One: Specifically formulate and define what you want from the transition and what your post transition needs will be. Think of this step as establishing your "destination".

Step Two: Establish your starting point. Where are you today, in both a practice and financial sense?

Step Three: Identify, and list in order of priority, your transition strategies. This is where you decide, given your resources, how you can get to your chosen destination. This could include practice building strategies, tax strategies, investment strategies, income management, and more. Incidentally, you've probably heard the expression, "Life is what happens while you're making other plans". I use this expression frequently in this book because it helps to bring home an important concept: the need for contingency planning strategies. Contingency planning may involve participating in a self-protection group, insurance, liquidity reserves, practice agreements and more.

Step Four: Break your long-term transition plan into 12-month Action Plans.

Step Five: Monitor your progress. This is critical. You must monitor your progress on a monthly or quarterly basis so that adjustments to the various aspects of your transition strategies can be made in a timely manner.

Step Six: Perform a yearly review and establish a new 12-month Action Plan that incorporates the previous five steps.

Over twenty years of experience and refinement have gone into the transition planning strategies explained in this book. Throughout the years, the dental practitioners with whom I've worked have found these strategies a successful template, and I trust you will too.

Managing a busy professional career, along with enjoying a rewarding personal life, takes good time-management skills. Out of respect for those skills, I've written this book using a streamlined format to ensure that the information is easy to understand and apply to your own personal situation. If you're acting as coach to your transition team, you'll find it provides a handy game plan.

One final comment. We're all individuals, and a good transition plan should be modified to realize your particular needs. One size fits all is not the best approach when it comes to your transition. In this book I discuss a system for planning your transition that has proven successful over the years. Some of the strategies mentioned in these pages will be right for your circumstances, and some of them won't. Therefore, it's very important that you check with your team of professional advisors when considering any of the strategies discussed within these pages.

Now let's begin....

CHAPTER ONE

SET SPECIFIC GOALS

This chapter will help you:

- Understand the importance of well-defined goals in transition planning

- Appreciate the value of prioritizing your goals

- Quantify your individual goals in current dollar terms

- See the impact of time as a variable in your goal setting

Your transition is a major milestone in your life. In a sense, you're the architect charged with the responsibility for the structure of your future. That's why it's so important that you plan for a transition that's right for you, as a unique individual.

In the Introduction, I outlined the Six Step Transition Planning Process that I've used with considerable success over the years. The first step in the process is **Formulating your Transition Goals** or, put another way, defining what you want from your transition. I recommend that this step also include a definition of your post transition needs, so that you end up with a complete picture of where you're headed.

BARRY'S COACHING ADVICE

Define what you want in a way that gives meaning to your ongoing strategies. Consider it a way to translate your dreams into your goals. Then think of your goals as the foundation upon which you build your strategies. Ultimately, it's by implementing your strategies that you get what you want. You shouldn't have goals without strategies. Strategies are the bridges that take you from where you are today to where you want to be tomorrow.

10 KEY STEPS IN FORMULATING YOUR TRANSITION GOALS

Below, I've summarized 10 key steps to help you formulate your goals and enhance the transition planning process.

Step 1: Goals Should Be Defined In Specific Terms

Successful goal setting is all about giving definition, shape, and structure to your dreams. When it comes to defining the transition you feel is right for you, there are many possibilities, variations and combinations from which to choose. Let's look at the pros and cons of some of the more common types of transitions.

1. Full Transition – Outside Purchaser

In this instance, you either exit immediately or work as an associate for a short period of time to facilitate the transfer of goodwill to the new dentist.

Pros:
- You get all your money out at one time.
- There's no continued staff or management responsibility.
- You pass on the responsibility and care of your patients quickly and efficiently.

Cons:
- Your change from a practicing dentist is very rapid, with no time to "ease into retirement".
- You lose any entitlement to future practice growth and profits.
- If you're in a small community or a specialty practice dependant on referrals, care should be taken to ensure that the sale of the practice is kept confidential until you have a firm purchase agreement in place.

2. Selling to a Cost Sharing Partner or a Full Partner

In this case, it's my experience that you get the best results when obtaining an independent third party valuation. You may also want to hire a facilitator as part of your transition team to work out the basic terms of the transition so that you'll be in a better position to instruct your lawyers and accountants on what you want.

Pros:
- You get all your money right away.
- Typically, you have a little more control on the timing of your exit from practice.
- You're relieved of staff and management responsibilities.

Cons:
- If you've practiced with someone for a long time, personal feelings and expectations can cloud important negotiation issues. In addition, some agreements that have been in place for awhile may have had buy-sell provisions that aren't appropriate in today's market place. For example, I worked with a client who had been in a partnership for over 30 years. When the client's health declined and he wanted to sell, we found that the old agreement stipulated that the buy-out price would be based on the value of the tangible assets only. When the agreement was put in place, goodwill had little real value. Sadly, his partners didn't want to recognize the fact that goodwill does have a value today. So avoid such disputes by keeping your practice agreements up to date.

3. Partial Transition to an Associate – Cost Sharing

In this type of transition an associate buys charts and a share of the office's tangible assets (equipment, leaseholds etc.). Generally, he or she is then entitled to all the revenue from their personal and hygiene production. Expenses are typically shared through a pre-set formula, such as each party pays an equal portion of fixed costs and a proportional share of variable costs based on production.

Pros:
- You may be able to slow down without a negative effect on the value of your practice.
- Some of your capital in the practice is freed up either for investment or some other worthwhile purpose that serves your longer-

term strategies.

- There is better coverage when you're on holidays.
- Management duties can be shared.
- You have the benefits of cooperative interaction.
- On a cost-sharing basis you have greater independence as compared to a partnership.
- Buy-sell arrangements can be put in place to protect the value of your practice from contingencies.
- You still get to enjoy the benefits and profits that come from practice ownership.
- There's a logical potential buyer for your remaining practice when you're ready to do a full transition.

Cons:

- You must consider another party when making decisions.
- There could be conflicts in practice philosophy, or other disagreements that aren't apparent before the associate has "bought in".
- You lose the benefit of profiting from the associate and hygiene production on the patient base that's purchased by him or her.

4. Partial Transition to an Associate – Partnership

Under a cost sharing arrangement, you have separate practices. A partnership is different in that only one practice exists. Basically, the members of a partnership work together and share everything including patient ownership and profits. There can be many formulas for the sharing of profits. They can be split on a 50% basis or even shared proportionately relative to production. Some partnerships work on a formula whereby they keep all of their personal revenue (less expenses) and the only sharing that's done is on hygiene and associate profits.

Pros:

- You spread out your financial risk because your partner(s) is/are there to share the investment and costs.
- There's better coverage when you're on holidays.
- Management duties can be shared.

- You have the benefits of cooperative interaction.
- Buy-sell arrangements can be put in place to protect the value of your partnership interest.
- You still get to enjoy the benefits and profits that come from practice ownership.
- There's a logical potential buyer for your remaining practice when you're ready to do a full transition.

Cons:
- As partners typically share everything, you have less flexibility for independent action. For example, you may be required to work a minimum number of days in the office or produce a minimum level of production.
- Resentment and potential conflicts can develop if one partner is not living up to the expectations of the other partners.
- Because of the close relationship of the parties, disagreements can be more stressful.
- While they're great when they work, partnerships don't have a good track record in the dental profession.

5. Partial Transition to an Associate – Charts only

Under this form of partial transition, an associate would be brought into the practice with the express understanding that he or she would buy their charts when they reached a minimum level (say 800 to 1,000) and move out of the office. In this variation, you would continue to benefit from the growth in your practice without having to give up any control and might even be able to slow down.

6. Merging your practice with a younger dentist

This concept works well if you have started to slow down and have reached a point where it's no longer practical, because of your declining patient load, to justify your own office and staff.

Moving in with a younger dentist who has some extra room often means that you can actively continue in practice. Often these arrangements are set up so that your overhead is all or mostly on a variable basis. In other words, rather than paying a fixed cost, you pay the younger dentist a percentage of production. In turn, he or she provides the facility, front-end staff, and perhaps the hygiene department.

I recommend you negotiate some kind of a purchase arrangement for your charts prior to moving in. It may be difficult to move out if you and the younger dentist can't agree on terms.

7. The "Fold your tent and walk" away transition

All too many dentists find themselves in this position. Typically they didn't address value management issues and have slowed down to the point where the practice no longer has any real value. They don't want to move in or merge with another practice. At the same time, production has dwindled to the point that it doesn't justify practicing. If you find yourself in this position, the hope is that you've set enough aside so that you have an adequate level of financial security. On one hand, you won't have to deal with the complications of selling your practice. On the other hand, it's a shame to have worked in your practice all those years and receive nothing for it at the end of the day.

In deciding what you want in a transition, ask yourself the following questions:

Q: What would be the ideal age for you to do a full transition?

Q: Would you consider a staged transition?

Q. If so, would you prefer a partnership, a cost sharing arrangement, just selling charts, or perhaps some other variation?

Q. What are you going to do with the extra time?

Q: Where would you live?

Q: Would you consider giving up your Canadian residence?

Q: Will you work in dentistry after your transition as an associate or locum? What about another career entirely? Full or part time?

Q: How much after-tax cash flow will you need to finance your ideal retirement lifestyle?

Let's take a closer look at that last question. You may find it difficult to estimate what your retirement lifestyle costs are going to be. As a guideline, consider what your lifestyle costs are today (a simple system called Banking By Objectives can be found later in this book to help you with this process). Then reduce this figure by expenditures that should be eliminated by that time, such as education and support for your children, debt service, some insurance costs and RRSPs. There also may be some cost estimates to be added. Examples would include an expensive hobby, travel plans, and an estimate for car replacement.

What you're trying to identify is your retirement lifestyle needs in today's dollars. This information, combined with estimates on time to transition, longevity, inflation, investment returns, taxation, details on your investable assets that relate to ownership and the ratio of RRSP to non RRSP investments, will make it possible for you and your transition team to quantify how much retirement capital you're going to need.

A qualified retirement planner should be one of the people in the team you enlist early in the pre-transition stage. He or she can perform the complex calculations you will require. To fulfill this important role, the planner must understand what strategy alternatives are available. They should understand how to estimate your needs, annuities, reverse mortgages, registered retirement income funds, how best to manage cash flow in retirement, when to encroach on capital, and so on.

The planner should also be comfortable dealing with estate-planning considerations. For this role, I recommend as a minimum, someone with a CFP designation (Certified Financial Planner) who has experience working with clients who are independent professionals and/or small business people. I also recommend that this vital member of your team work on a fee for service basis as opposed to being compensated by way of commission earned from the products they sell. I'm not saying that people who make their living on a commission aren't capable or ethical. It's simply that there are important decisions that will be based on the expertise of this valuable member of your transition team, and you want to be certain that the recommendations they are making are motivated by what is in your best interest.

In the next chapter, we'll be discussing what I call your *Current Position*. Having determined the amount of money you're going to need to finance your retirement, you'll be able to see whether or not your current resources are sufficient or if you'll need to build additional wealth—and how much. Here again the experienced retirement planner should provide valuable input. They should be able to tell you whether or not your resources are sufficient to provide for your future needs. If you need to save more or create more wealth, they should be able to tell you exactly how much and ideally how to go about it. We'll look at this topic again in later chapters.

Step 2: Your Transition Goals Should Be Realistic

Setting realistic attainable goals is quite motivating. They can invigorate you and provide more purpose to your day. Such goals can even enhance the satisfaction you feel from working when you see yourself achieving these objectives. Setting goals that are *not* realistic can and usually do have the opposite effect. They're nothing more than a recipe for frustration.

Why would a goal be unrealistic? Well, from a financial perspective it has to do with what is called a "resource gap". In other words, you don't have the money, assets or earning ability to get where you want to go. That's why the next chapter, Establishing Your Current Position, is so important. It will help you develop a good understanding of what your financial resources are today. After all, ***you need good information to make good decisions.*** Knowing where you are today is a prerequisite to developing workable transition strategies for tomorrow.

Step 3: Prioritize your goals

Unless you expect to inherit great wealth, you probably have finite financial resources. That means you have to focus those resources on what you have identified as your most important goals. Sounds easy, doesn't it?

The difficulty arises when you have to select what goals are "most important". I recommend you set no more than three to five prioritized goals. Having too many goals can dilute your focus.

Step 4: Break down goals into appropriate components

You have no doubt heard the old adage, "How do you eat an elephant? One bite at a time". Most big goals can be broken down into components that make them easy to relate to and achieve.

To be useful in setting transition strategies, financial objectives need to be broken down in a meaningful way. For example, let's assume your planning indicates that you'll need to increase gross production by $30,000 per year. Expressed in this manner, this may seem like a daunting objective. On the other hand, if you work 220 days per year, this is only an extra $136.36 per day. It's far easier to come up with strategies to increase production by this amount, as opposed to the larger annual goal.

Here's another example. Assume that you have to save $25,000 per year over and above RRSPs to build the wealth you'll need for your transition. It must also be assumed that you have the discretionary cash to meet this objective. Otherwise, we'd be back to strategies to increase production as described in the previous example. By discretionary cash, I mean after-tax funds that aren't committed. After all, you can't decide to stop paying for normal day to day living needs, debts, etc. Discretionary funds are those monies about which you can make choices. Once again, it is difficult to take action on a large goal such as this. Breaking this figure down to a more manageable level, such as savings of $500 per week or $2,083 per month, is the secret to turning financial goals into reality.

Step 5: Integrate your practice and personal goals

If you're like most dentists, your practice is the engine that drives your financial train. This is where you earn your personal income. I consider the following a Golden Rule of dental financial management: *Your practice must either support your personal needs, or your personal needs must be adapted to what the practice can support.*

When dentists run into financial trouble, it's often because they didn't integrate their practice and personal planning. If you decide to spend money on office renovations, it'll affect the cash flow you have available for personal use. If you decide to renovate your home, the money generally must come from your practice.

BARRY'S COACHING ADVICE

 Your personal financial life and your practice are intimately linked. Therefore, it's prudent not to commit to strategies in one part of your life without making sure they complement the other.

Step 6: Put your goals in writing

Unfortunately, memory is short and easily distorted. To illustrate my point, let me recall an experiment we did in elementary school. The teacher (who had one of those disrespectful nicknames that only young kids can come up with) whispered a statement into the ear of one of the children. The idea was that each child would then whisper it into the ear of the classmate next to him or her until everyone in the room had heard it. The interesting thing about this experiment is that the statement whispered into the ear of the last child was nothing like the one the teacher first passed on. It became distorted in the telling.

Putting your goals in writing is the best way to avoid this kind of distortion. It formalizes the process and cements the commitment. If in the course of time you forget how your goals are prioritized or a specific detail about any of them, you can simply refer to the written word. Committing your goals to paper also facilitates the measurement of your progress (or lack thereof) over a period of time. In addition to describing the goal in writing, I recommend that you include the strategy and the timeframe. If others will be responsible for carrying out a part of the strategy, make a note of that, also.

Step 7: Communicate your goals to other interested parties

Dentistry takes teamwork. Therefore, if your goals involve the practice, the specifics should be communicated to your team, with the understanding that you don't have to reveal personal details or share private information. For example, if you and your advisors determine that you need to produce an additional $300 per day to reach your objective this year, you would simply share this objective with them. This will help them take on some of the responsibility and "buy into" the goal. It will also help you define your expectations and you'll know when they're doing a great job and when they're not.

Naturally, it's also a good idea to fully involve the home team in your goals. It strengthens commitment and ideally enlists the whole family in reaching the objectives.

Step 8: Strategies and goals should be reviewed and revised regularly

Consider setting aside what I call 'B' time to review at least biannually your progress and strategies. 'B' time is the time you take to handle those important activities that aren't urgent. If your strategies involve increasing gross production, I suggest reviewing it more frequently – say quarterly.

Monitoring your progress is critically important! The best time to find out that you're *not* meeting your goal is when corrective action can still be taken. Waiting until the end of the year to find out that you didn't make your income targets leaves you without any options. However, if you find out in the first quarter of the year that you're not on target, it's still possible to make adjustments to achieve your objective.

In addition to monitoring your progress, you can use a 'B' day late in the year for an in-depth review. Doing so will allow you to incorporate what happened during the past year, as well as the outlook for the coming year, so that you can establish new meaningful goals for the next 12-month period. You may even find that your goals have changed. Or you may have decided you would like to try a staged transition where an associate is brought in on the basis that they'll be buying part of the practice. If you were unable to find a suitable candidate or if you entered into an arrangement that didn't work, then you may want to change your transition goal to a full transition model.

There could be other changes, too. You may decide that you need more money for your retirement living needs, taxes may have changed, or the economic outlook. The point is, by reviewing your goals and strategies regularly, you're able to modify them in a timely manner so that you reach your ultimate objective.

Step 9: Make contingency plans

In planning for the future the expression, "Life is what happens while you're making other plans" should be taken to heart. No one knows what challenges the future will bring. That's why it's important to make sure you have emergency funds available for things like home and auto repairs and the necessary replacement of office equipment.

For larger contingencies, make sure you have appropriate amounts of life insurance, disability insurance, office overhead insurance, and personal property and liability coverage. Critical illness is another form of coverage you may want to consider. It's also advisable to make contingency plans to protect the goodwill in your practice.

Step 10: Consider the non-financial implications of your transition

A successful transition from your practice to retirement will require more than just an orderly disposition of the practice and the financial wherewithal to support a comfortable lifestyle.

When you think about it, there will be upwards of 2000 hours of time to fill in a year. Unless you plan how to use this time in a rewarding and satisfying manner, your retirement may be a disappointment. Studies show that retirement can have a deep emotional impact which could affect your health, marriage and other relationships, even your lifespan.

The practitioners who are most successful with this aspect of their life's transition are those who approach it the way they approached their practice. Being happy and contented in retirement takes effort! I can't tell you how many clients have confided to me, a year or two after retirement, about how much they miss the practice. They had great visions of playing golf, relaxing down south in the winter, and spending time at the cottage in the summer. But the reality is that golf is great as a hobby or an escape, but you can only play so many games a year (or at least that's true for some of us). Also, relaxing down south can get pretty boring after a period of time unless you have a satisfying activity to use up all the energy that used to go into your practice. Therefore, you may want to add a lifeplanner to your transition team.

I hope I've impressed upon you how important it is to formalize your goals and strategies. It's the first step down the road to your future happiness, and if you get off on the right foot, you'll find the journey easier and more enjoyable.

CHAPTER TWO

ESTABLISH YOUR CURRENT POSITION

PART ONE: CASH FLOW

This chapter will help you:

- Understand the importance of Cash Flow

- Know how much money is available from your practice to finance your personal needs

- Know how to figure out your Personal Living Expenses (PLE)

- Work with your transition advisory team to establish this key transition planning information

The starting line

Where are you today, in a financial sense, relative to your transition and retirement goals? The hope is that you've built up assets, such as a valuable practice, RRSPs, and other savings. But will it be enough? Or will you need to set aside more money, and if so, how much? To answer these important questions, you must first understand what your financial resources are likely to be over the next 12 months. I call this, Establishing your Current Position. Think of this initial process as the starting line for your transition planning.

Let me draw an analogy between the importance of determining your Current Position and having the information you need to prepare an effective treatment plan for a patient. Before you design a treatment plan, you must first ensure that you have a thorough understanding of the patient's present oral health and overall physical condition. The same is true for a meaningful transition plan. It's vital that you understand your present financial health for the planning period in question, or in other words, your Current Position.

Establishing your Current Position requires that you understand two general categories of information. The first is your Cash Flow: What money comes in and what money goes out. The second is your Net Worth: What you have and what you owe in terms of assets and liabilities. We'll cover Net Worth in the next chapter, so first let's turn to Cash Flow.

The importance of Cash Flow

The greatest financial resource that most dentists have is their Cash Flow. (I'm assuming that you didn't win the lottery or won't inherit great wealth in the near future.) To put the importance of your Cash Flow into perspective, consider the following example. If your practice is currently grossing $600,000 per year, and you have 10 years to a full transition, assuming inflation will average 3% you can expect to have a total inflow during this period of $6,878,327. That's a lot of money going through your hands – money that you'll have to make decisions about, such as how to best use it.

Cash flow is an important resource, but it's typically not well understood. This is unfortunate because if you can't understand it, you can't manage it! In fact, understanding the practice component of this valuable resource is fairly straightforward. There are many established systems that can tell you what happens to your income and expenses at the office (practice statements and tax returns). But from then on, it's a Black Hole as far as reliable information is concerned. Don't worry though. As you'll see, there's a simple way to develop the attention to detail that you'll need to understand what happens to your cash. The place to start is with your practice.

First however, let me put your mind at ease. You don't have to be a mathematician, accountant, or MBA to establish your Current Position or figure out your Cash Flow or Net Worth. You'll probably just need to know how to direct the appropriate members of your advisory team, and make sure they have the right information to make the right decisions. On the other hand, if you're preparing your own Current Position you'll find the following information useful in guiding you through the process.

Fundamentally, to develop the Cash Flow component of your Current Position you would use historical information, which we'll discuss in a moment, combined with your expectations of what's going to happen over the next 12 months.

Step 1: What money comes in and what money goes out: Your practice

At this stage, we want to know how much money is available on a pre-tax basis from the practice to finance your personal needs. For dentists, Cash Flow starts with the practice gross. Gross collections represent your inflow of funds. Expenses, excluding non-cash expenses, make up your practice outflow. Non-cash expenses include amortization or depreciation. This is an allowance provided for in the Tax Act that recognizes that the value of your tangible assets, such as equipment, declines over time or with use. Think of it as a deduction that reduces taxable income, without you *directly* having to pay out any money.

Unincorporated Practices

For an unincorporated practice, where there are no corporations in place, the process is simple. I suggest for reference that you use your most recent year end profit and loss statement, or as it's often referred to, your *Income and Expense Statement*. This document is historical in nature, so where appropriate make any adjustments for the present year. To do this, ask yourself the following questions:

Q: *Will gross production be the same, higher or lower?*

Q: *What will change from an expense perspective? If you anticipate a change in gross production, don't forget to make a corresponding adjustment to variable expenses (dental supplies, lab and so on).*

Q: Will any leases mature?

Q: Did you hire any more staff?

Q: Have any other costs gone up or down?

Q: Do you plan to buy any equipment or incur any capital expenditures in the practice over the next 12 months?

By deducting estimated expenses from your anticipated gross production, you should have a pretty good estimate of what is available to you in terms of pretax Cash Flow.

Incorporated practices

Corporations, as they relate to Current Position, are in some ways only another entity for tax purposes. This is important to understand. Money earned in the corporation doesn't automatically fall into your personal income for tax or Cash Flow purposes, as does the net from an unincorporated practice. Earnings in a corporation may not necessarily be paid out in the present year. Some dental families accumulate earnings not needed for their personal lifestyle in their companies. It's a good place to save money for your goals. (We'll look at this concept in more detail in the Tax Strategies chapter). Nonetheless, it's still a financial resource that's at your disposal. Think of it as having your funds in different pockets, with the corporation simply being another pocket.

Step 2: Personal Cash Inflow: What comes in

Summarize all net income sources, including:

- net practice income
- income your spouse earned, through the practice, or other employment
- non-cash expenses, if available, from your unincorporated practice
- dividends
- anticipated interest income proceeds of any borrowings personally or in an unincorporated practice

- any other inflow of funds should also be included, such as gifts, proceeds from the sale of property, and so on

Step 3: Cash Outflow – What goes out

Income Tax – Definitely in the Outflow category

Ask your financial advisor or accountant to calculate the tax for you. He or she will need details about your income expectations for the coming period. Computer programs are so sophisticated today that given the right information, your financial advisor/accountant should be able to work out a figure suitable for planning purposes in minutes. A simple Cash Flow management and monitoring system I've used effectively with many clients is called Banking By Objectives (BBO), and it's described below. By the way, if you're making quarterly tax payments, you may want to set up a tax account within your BBO system, so that you can deposit funds on a monthly basis.

Personal Lifestyle Expenditures (PLE)

Don't be concerned if you don't immediately know what your personal lifestyle expenditures are or how to go about calculating them. You're not alone. Most people would be hard pressed to provide anything other than a rough estimate (that's often not even close) if asked to come up with this figure.

Perhaps you share my view that the most important money you have is what's left over after practice expenses. This is the money that finances your lifestyle, educates your children, and builds your future financial security. So understanding your PLE is critical. Once again, let me say, "*If you can't understand it, you can't manage it!*"

As just mentioned, PLE includes all expenditures for your lifestyle. A little further on in this chapter we'll look at some simple systems for identifying these numbers. Please be aware that I'm not asking you to prepare a budget. In today's society the word 'budget' has negative connotations, the same way the word 'diet' does. Very few people enjoy the idea of a constraining personal budget. So, you'll be happy to hear that the answer to controlling your finances and reaching your objectives is not cutting back on your personal lifestyle. If it turns out that you don't have the Cash Flow or other resources necessary to meet your goals and expectations, the most successful solutions have proven to be increasing net revenue in the practice or changing, perhaps marginally, your goals or time frames.

But first we have to understand what it costs to finance your lifestyle in order to evaluate whether or not your revenue is adequate for all your needs. Having this information is critical to taking control of your financial future. Such control can only come with strategies that are appropriate for your individual circumstances.

PLE represents funds that you've committed to paying out. It doesn't include discretionary expenditures or savings. It's similar to Fixed Expenses in your office, and examples include food, shelter and transportation costs, along with expenditures for your children's needs, loan payments, and insurance premiums for *necessary* coverage.

BARRY'S COACHING ADVICE

PLE should also include clothing, entertainment, vacations, and even pocket money for you and your spouse. With respect to pocket money, ideally your PLE should provide sufficient money so that you and your spouse can meet your personal spending needs without being accountable to each other for how the money is spent.

How to determine and manage your PLE

There are many ways to determine your PLE, and some are more involved than others. Over the years, I've experimented with them all. One important point: this is not something you can effectively delegate to your transition advisory team.

If you like working with a computer, and you have the time to do the data entry, software programs can do the job extremely well. However it can be challenging to come home from a busy day at the office and spend an hour or two entering details of your personal and household accounts into a software program.

Another way you can determine your PLE is through a system I call Banking By Objectives (BBO). This system allows you to identify your money with its intended use, which is part of the reason it's successful as a Cash Flow monitoring system. In fact, it's the system my mother used when I was a young child. I remember that she always had wrinkled beige envelopes in her purse. They went everywhere she did. Eventually I discovered how effectively she used them. You see, there were things she wanted or needed for either herself or the family, and to manage the saving process she created this system of envelopes. She had separate envelopes for house repairs, vacations, clothes and so on. She identified the money contained in those envelopes with its purpose and whenever she wanted to know how she was doing on that priority, she simply pulled out the envelope and counted the contents. Certainly, there are more sophisticated systems for managing your cash. On the other hand, her's worked — and worked simply. She would consistently reach her goal.

Banking By Objectives is based on this system. It's a simple feedback system that can also be enlarged to encompass other priorities, such as taxes. To use Banking By Objectives to establish your PLE, follow these two steps:

Step One: Go through your chequebooks and credit card bills for the past 12 months. Remove any non-recurring discretionary items. Are there any personal expenses that you've paid through the office by credit card? At the end of the year your accountant would typically allocate these expenditures to your personal draw, so these funds are definitely part of your PLE. They should be factored in as well. To this amount add any anticipated increases in expenditures. For example, has your mortgage payment gone up? Did you lease a new car? Perhaps your house taxes decreased – OK, that's unlikely!

Now you're ready to divide this total figure by 12 for a general idea of your average monthly PLE. This is the figure you would initially use in your Current Position, discussed in the next chapter. Now, because it's difficult to determine this figure with any real accuracy, you can also use the BBO system to confirm your assumptions as outlined below.

Step Two: Confirm your PLE estimate. As just mentioned, the BBO system can do that for you. Just set up or designate an existing bank account as your PLE account and arrange for it to be covered by overdraft protection. Now, let's say your review of chequebooks and credit card statements indicated that you spend $7,000 per month on PLE. For the next year, deposit into the PLE account (using any time schedule that's convenient) from the practice account or your professional corporation this $7,000 per month. All identified PLE outflows should then be paid for from this account. Don't take the money for any PLE item from any other account. Even credit cards used for items that would be categorized as PLE expenses should be paid from here.

Now you have a simple feedback system!

If your PLE account is always going into overdraft, you'll know how much your initial estimate was out. Or conversely, if a surplus builds up, you'll know how to adjust your PLE estimate.

By establishing your realistic PLE, it should also be possible to determine how much money, if any, you have left over. To arrive at this important number, deduct your PLE and the income tax estimate from your total anticipated inflow for the year. I refer to what's left over as your Discretionary Cash, and it's generally very small in relation to the amount of money that has flowed through your hands from all sources. Yet, it's still important because this is the only money you can really make decisions upon. After all, you can't decide to stop paying staff salaries or suppliers at the office. Nor can you stop paying for food, clothes or shelter. For the most part you're committed to many expenses before you even earn the money at chairside.

Identifying your level of Discretionary Cash (or the lack of it) is critical to sound transition planning. Your resources are finite. When you don't identify your level of Discretionary Cash, it is easy to spend it on secondary priorities, often on impulse. In the last chapter we talked about goals. By identifying the cost of those goals, Discretionary Cash can be allocated from the outset towards achieving them. That means you're taking care of your essential priorities first. From that point on, you can spend the rest of your income knowing that you've already taken care of your most important priorities.

CHAPTER THREE

ESTABLISH YOUR CURRENT POSITION

PART TWO: NET WORTH

This chapter will help you:

- Know the uses of a Net Worth Statement and how it's prepared
- Understand the importance of classifying your assets and liabilities by type and ownership
- Appreciate the connection between your Cash Flow and Net Worth
- Be aware of valuation terms and methods as they relate to your practice
- Know how often your Net Worth Statement should be updated

In the last chapter we discussed your Current Position as a starting point for your transition planning. Your starting point can be thought of as a two-sided coin. On one side of the Current Position coin you have Cash Flow – dealt with in the last chapter – and on the other side you have Net Worth, which details what you have and what you owe.

Think of Net Worth and Cash Flow as being linked together in a dynamic sense. Any Cash Flow you generate after tax that isn't spent on perishables (items without lasting value) will impact your Net Worth. For example, money spent on vacations or dining out may provide great personal value, but unfortunately they won't add to your asset base as represented by your Net Worth. On the other hand, Cash Flow used to purchase a house, car, investments, or to build a savings account will affect your Net Worth. These are tangible assets. When you use your Cash Flow to acquire tangible items, you're simply changing the character of a resource from a very liquid tradeable commodity to another form of asset. Long lasting financial security and wealth can only be built when part of your hard-earned Cash Flow has an impact on your Net Worth.

Your Net Worth Statement

No doubt you have heard the expression "a picture is worth a 1000 words", and in my experience that's definitely the case when trying to understand a client's assets and liabilities. I find it useful to think of a client's Net Worth as just that, a picture or a snapshot of what you have and what you owe *at a particular point in time*. This preparation of a Net Worth has the possibility of not only revealing some interesting and exciting financial features, but is a critical part of establishing your Current Position or starting point for planning purposes.

The picture your Net Worth Statement reflects is really what you have to show for all your hard work over the years. It's called a Net Worth Statement because deducting your liabilities (what you owe), from your assets (what you have), tells you how much you're worth in dollar terms, on a net basis. Your Net Worth picture can provide vital information for your transition. Let's take a quick look at three specific ways it can help you.

1. It can help you understand the present makeup of your Net Worth

When you do a full transition, at some future point you'll be dependent on the Cash Flow that your assets will generate to finance your lifestyle needs. It's important to look at the distribution of the assets that make up your Net Worth. What you need to do is establish what are potential revenue-producing assets and what are not. Let's look at an example of why this is important.

Dentist A has a Net Worth of $1,500,000 with 30% of the assets of a personal use nature (and unlikely to generate cash flow after transition).

Dentist B has a Net Worth of $2,000,000 with 60% of the assets categorized as personal or non-producing.

Question: Which dentist has greater financial security, assuming lifestyle needs are similar?

Answer: Dentist A. What counts is not only how large your Net Worth is, but rather how well it's organized relative to your needs and goals.

BARRY'S COACHING ADVICE

 If a large portion of your Net Worth is invested in a house and you're planning, as part of your transition, to sell it and move into a less expensive place, I'd advise caution. In all my years of working with dentists, I've seen very few cases where this strategy has proved to work satisfactorily.

2. It can facilitate long term tax planning

Income splitting and tax deferral options are cornerstones of tax planning in Canada. How investable assets are split between spouses, the relative weighting of registered assets (RRSPs/pensions), non-registered assets, corporate assets, etc. can all have an impact on how much tax you pay. It's ideal to have a mix of assets that have different tax consequences when living off the income and/or capital. I'll cover this topic in more detail in a later chapter. For now let me say that whether you're preparing your own Net Worth or having it prepared through your advisory team, make sure your assets are categorized by type and ownership (what's in each spouse's name or joint title). Doing so will be useful to you and your advisors in planning strategies for both your transition and eventual retirement.

3. It can provide a tool to measure your financial progress

Let's assume that a year ago you prepared your first Current Position as part of a long-range transition plan. Your goals, based on Cash Flow expectations at that time, were to save $2,000 per month beyond RRSP contributions for your financial security, $300 per month for your child's education via an RESP, and to reduce your debt by about 20%. It's now 12 months later. The only way to know whether or not you should be congratulating yourself for accomplishing your objectives is to compare your present Net Worth Statement to the one you prepared a year ago. It's also the only way you can properly gauge the impact of returns or losses on your existing investment assets in relation to your overall financial security. Let me add another example. Suppose, when you first prepared your Net Worth, it was apparent that the available investment assets of one spouse were substantially greater than the other. This is not a desirable position for tax planning purposes. Your savings strategy at the time would likely have been to build up that additional wealth in the name of the spouse with the lower investment base (see the section on tax planning). Did the strategy of using an updated Net Worth Statement to measure your progress work or didn't it?

How often should a Net Worth Statement be prepared?

A new Net Worth Statement should be prepared every 12 months – at a minimum. Why so often? Because you need to monitor your progress. The other practical reason for this frequency is that you and one or more members of your advisory team will have to prepare a new 12-month plan for the coming year. In effect you're creating a new starting line. The secret to accomplishing a long-term objective is to break down the actions that must be taken into "edible bites". Similarly, a long-term transition plan is best accomplished with a series of 12-month action plans that move you toward your objective.

When you and the appropriate advisory team members do your comparison with the Net Worth Statement prepared last year, you may find that your Net Worth grew more or less than expected. Perhaps some investment returns were better or worse than expected, or you had expenses that lowered your savings, or maybe you earned more than you anticipated and your savings were greater than planned. It's unlikely you would find everything worked out exactly as expected. Transition planning is dealing with the future, which none of us can see with any real clarity. You have to constantly make adjustments to allow for the unexpected. Preparing this picture of your assets and liabilities at least every 12 months will help you know what adjustments need to be made for the following year's plan.

A Net Worth Statement is therefore a vital part of establishing your Current Position or starting line because it provides you with information that's critical to the success of your transition strategies. I can't stress enough the importance of completing and utilizing this financial tool effectively.

Preparing your Net Worth Statement

Here are some steps to guide you through the process.

Step One: Pick a date

Remember that your Net Worth is a snapshot of what you have and what you owe *at a particular point in time.* The date you choose (in consultation with your advisors) should be the same day each year. I recommend you select a date where information will be readily available, as opposed to some arbitrary time line. An example would be December 31, or if you have a non-calendar fiscal year end for your practice, that date would also be suitable.

Step Two: Organize your information

You'll have to assemble your "stuff" on your chosen date. By "stuff" I mean:

- all bank statements (practice, corporate, & personal)
- investment statements
- confirmation of outstanding balances on debt
- value estimates for your practice
- value estimates for real estate
- actual cash surrender value (after all redemption charges and penalties) of whole life or universal life contracts
- values on other assets such as limited partnerships, non-dental active business interests, art, stamp or coin collections, and so on

In some cases, accurate values may not be immediately available. While it's important to get this information right, keep in mind that you're not preparing audited financial statements. If the information is not available, that doesn't mean you can't proceed. In some cases you have to make estimates. Do the best you can with the information available. If accurate details aren't available, make your estimates on the conservative side.

When it comes to other personal use assets such as furnishings, cars or boats, simply make an estimate of their value. They have little or no impact on transition planning because they don't appreciate in value and will never generate any income.

Step Three: Complete your Net Worth form or have it completed for you

Once you've accumulated the data or "stuff" you'll need, you can begin completing the Net Worth form. If you're having it prepared by a member of your advisory team, make sure they understand how you want the information organized. It would also be wise to agree on a deadline for its completion. A new Cash Flow projection should be prepared at the same time.

Defining some categories

Most of the asset categories are self-explanatory, but some require additional comments for clarity.

Cash. This category doesn't include registered (RRSP/ Pension) or corporate cash. Cash in your RRSP or corporation normally can't be withdrawn without tax consequences. Technically, cash would be allocated to reserves for emergencies, or expenditures that are anticipated within the next 12 months. This is also a good place to track uncommitted cash that has accumulated. This category doesn't include cash reserves that may form part of your long-term investment portfolio, as these funds are committed to a longer-term purpose. It would be recorded therefore as a part of your registered or non-registered investment assets. All you are trying to identify are the cash reserves that are available for liquidity purposes.

The Practice. If you have had a valuation prepared recently by a qualified practice valuator, then you would enter that figure. A professional valuation is the most accurate way to determine what your practice is worth on the market. Some professional valuators offer an update service that you may find advantageous, particularly if you're within five years of transition. The update is annual and the cost is nominal compared to a new valuation.

If you haven't had a professional valuation prepared (my recommended course of action), there is a method I use for deciding on what figure to note on a client's Net Worth Statement for the practice. Let me stress that this is not an opinion of value in the traditional sense. Many factors go into determining the Fair Market Value (FMV) of a practice for sale purposes. Rather, this is a way of trying to identify what the practice is worth to you, the owner, as an investment. FMV can also be useful as an ongoing measure of value management in planning practice transition strategies.

The calculation involves "capitalizing" the net earnings of the practice. In brief, you take the net, normalized profits *(explained later)* that the practice generates, and divide it by a factor that compensates you for both the risk level you undertake in practice ownership and for the lack of liquidity. To illustrate this point, consider an investment that's generating a profit of $40,000 per year. If you wanted to earn 12% on your money, how much would you pay for the right to receive this $40,000 per year? The answer is simple. Divide $40,000 by 12% ($40,000/.12). The price you would pay in order to get 12% on your capital would be $333,333. To confirm the accuracy of this calculation, multiply $333,333 by 12%. If you felt there was a greater risk of receiving this $40,000 per year, you might demand a greater return in order to induce you to invest.

Doing the math

I recommend the appropriate member of your advisory team perform this calculation. To understand the process, the value estimate for purposes of your net worth would generally be calculated as follows:

Step One: First normalize the practice operating results (on a consolidated basis if you have a hygiene or technical services company) by taking the profits from your financial statement and adding back the following:

- Tax planning, such as salary to a spouse or children over what you would have paid an arms length person for the same work
- Lease payments or financing costs, because whether or not you have invested cash or financing you are liable for what is invested in your practice. What we're trying to determine is the real return on that capital
- Allowances for personal expenses, such as your car, personal travel, unusually high continuing education costs, etc.

Step Two: From this adjusted profit calculated in step one would be deducted: a factor for your personal production, typically 40%. You basically have two things that are at work in your practice – you and your capital. Keep in mind that the value we are trying to determine relates to the return on your capital, *not* on your personal production. To make an accurate assessment of real profit, there has to be some recognition of the fact that part of your time, as a practice owner, must be devoted to management in addition to production. This can be difficult to measure. You could take your hourly production rate and keep track of how many hours you have to spend weekly and/or monthly on management related activities. You would then multiply that figure by your hourly production rate to assess a logical management allowance. But this requires a lot of time and effort. Instead, you might want to simply take 3% of gross (net of laboratory costs) for a small practice and up to 5% of gross (net of laboratory) for a larger practice.

If you're professionally incorporated, use this same capitalization concept. After all, you're not preparing an actual valuation but rather trying to determine what the practice is worth to you right now as an investment.

Hygiene or Technical Services Corporations (TSC). If you have a hygiene company or TSC owned by your spouse and/or a trust for your children, the value of any non-practice tangible assets such as investments or cash would be noted only.

Cash Surrender Value of life insurance. Another entry that may require some explanation is the Cash Surrender Value (CSV) of life insurance. Have your agent provide you with a letter advising what the actual CSV is as of the date you've chosen to prepare your Net Worth Statement. It's important to define CSV as the amount you would receive if you asked for a cheque. Insurance contracts and terms can be complex. I've seen many policies that state that the owner's CSV is subject to redemption charges and/or surrender charges – and these charges can be significant. This is particularly true of policies that have been in force under five years. I recently had a client ask what his CSV was on his policy. He was told that it was $29,000. He then asked whether this was the amount of the cheque he would receive. It wasn't. The actual amount of the cheque would be $1,500. This is a big difference that can impact your savings plans and investment strategies.

Some Rules of Thumb for Net Worth

Rules of Thumb are general guidelines, so please consider these comments accordingly:

Rule 1: If you have any non-deductible debt, make paying it off a priority. There are no investments of which I'm aware that can provide as good a return, after-tax, with no risk, as paying off non-deductible debt. For example, if you have a non-deductible loan at 7%, assuming a top marginal tax rate of about 46% (in Ontario), you would have to get a pre-tax rate of return equal to 13.21%. Where can you get an investment with that kind of return and **no risk** in today's world? To pay off $5,000 of non-deductible debt you have to earn, on a pre-tax basis in the practice, assuming 20% variable costs, about $11,111. Ideally part of your transition plan should be the elimination of all debt, but particularly non-deductible debt prior to your transition.

Rule 2: If your debt level, whether deductible or not, is 40% or greater than your asset base, I strongly recommend that you concentrate your resources on reducing it.

BARRY'S COACHING ADVICE

 If you have extensive debt relative to your assets, run, don't walk, to a qualified financial planner or accountant– anyone who does more than tax returns and financial statements – for immediate help!

Rule 3: Build levels of liquidity (cash reserves) to the point where they will cover at least six months of living expenses plus any major purchases during the six-month period. This provides the security to meet most contingencies not covered by insurance. Many dentists I know feel they don't need to worry about reserves because they have available lines of credit. Maintaining enough cash to handle anticipated purchases is a good way to manage your spending. Don't accumulate non-deductible debt that will hinder your transition planning.

Rule 4: If you have tax arrears, consider borrowing the money to bring you current. Even if the borrowing will be non-deductible, the costs will be lower than what the Canada Customs and Revenue Agency charges.

Rule 5: If you have credit card debt that can't be paid off monthly, borrow from the bank to repay your high rates of interest balance.

Rule 6: Where possible, if you have non-deductible debt as well as deductible debt, have all principal repayment directed to the non-deductible debt and arrange for the deductible liability to be on an interest-only basis until there are no longer any non-deductible obligations.

Rule 7: Many of the books written on financial advice today recommend that you build the RRSP levels for each spouse so they are equal in value. This advice is reasonable as a general rule for the majority of the population. When it comes to a dental family, it would be preferable to make sure that the total amount of investable assets, including an allocation for the proceeds of your practice sale, are balanced between spouses. In many cases there can be a great disparity between the income of the dentist and the spouse. The result can be that investable assets build up disproportionately in the name of the dental spouse. That is not ideal from a transition planning perspective (see chapter on tax planning).

Once you've had your Net Worth Statement properly prepared, you will be well on your way to determining your Current Position or starting line. On a practical level you'll have an excellent understanding of how your assets and liabilities are organized. Plus, you'll have a useful tool for establishing strategies, addressing problem areas and tax planning, and measuring your progress. Ideally, establishing your Net Worth should leave you feeling empowered and ready for the next step in planning your transition.

CHAPTER FOUR

TRANSITION STRATEGIES

PART ONE: AN INTRODUCTION

This chapter will help you:

- Understand the difference between Wealth Creation and Wealth Management

- Know how to determine which strategies are best suited to your unique circumstances

When approaching transition strategies, it may help to build a mental image of them as bridges that take you from where you are today to where you want to be in the future. That's why in the preceding chapters emphasis was placed on goal setting and establishing where, in a financial sense, you are today. Knowing where you are now and where you want to go puts you in a powerful position. It equips you to create effective strategies and bridges to a future that's right for you.

Wealth Creation and Wealth Management

It's important to differentiate between Wealth Creation on the one hand, and Wealth Management on the other. Most of us think of the word "wealth" as a term that applies to the very rich. That's not the case in this context. The definition used here relates to an individual's or family's assets of a non-personal nature. That excludes the house for example, the car or home furnishings, and other assets of that nature. Let's look at some definitions to make things clearer.

Wealth Creation involves actions that create or harness the Cash Flow you need so that it can be organized strategically to meet your defined goals.

Wealth Management involves strategies which are intended to ensure that what you have is optimized and protected from losses that can occur through undertaking greater risk than necessary, inflation, taxation, or lack of focus. Depending on your individual Current Position or your starting point, your strategies may emphasize Wealth Management alone, or Wealth Management in combination with Wealth Creation. All of the strategies discussed in this chapter fall into one or the other of these two categories.

Wealth Creation and Wealth Management strategies are most effective when they're properly coordinated to complement each other. In the dental profession, Wealth Creation for most dentists is centred on the practice. Wealth Management complements your Wealth Creation activities in the practice. The whole purpose of Wealth Management strategies is to optimize what you have and to maintain the integrity of the capital or relative wealth that you've built up. It makes no sense to have effective Wealth Creation strategies if the money is lost.

What best applies in your situation: Wealth Creation or Wealth Management?

After defining and quantifying your goals (See Step 1 in the chapter on Goal Setting) and determining your Current Position, you'll be in one of the following three positions:

POSITION 1) You **do** have sufficient capital today to meet your identified needs and goals given reasonable assumptions. This definition includes either having the funds today or the asset base, which, if left to grow, would reasonably be expected to reach the required level. Of course, this is the best of all possible scenarios. If this describes your situation, you should be emphasizing Wealth Management. Wealth Management strategies are a combination of practice and income management, tax planning, investment strategy, and risk management (insurance, estate planning, practice agreements, practice contingency plans). It's also important that you monitor your position to make sure nothing happens to change this outlook.

POSITION 2) If your capital today were invested, it would likely **not** grow to the point that your assessments have identified as being necessary. However, you and/or your advisors have calculated that you **do** have the discretionary levels of cash needed to meet identified savings. Keep in mind that discretionary cash simply means that you have after-tax income that's not spoken for in advance. In other words, you don't require this money for things such as lifestyle needs, debt repayment, educating your children, and so on. Without some form of disciplined savings plan in place, discretionary funds tend to be spent on secondary priorities or impulse purchases. Overall, if you're in this situation, employ a combination of Wealth Creation and Wealth Management strategies.

POSITION 3) You **don't** have either the asset base or the discretionary cash today to meet your identified objective. Many dentists find themselves in this position. If you find that you fall into this category, don't be disheartened. There are alternatives. When you first assess your Current Position relative to your long-term objectives, it can be a real eye-opener. I've also heard it referred to as a 'wake up call'. Should you find yourself in this position your choices are:

> a) **Create the additional wealth you need.** This would be done through a combination of improving the practice bottom line, emphasizing proactive tax planning (see Tax Planning chapter), income management, and savings strategies. I didn't include 'improving investment returns' as one of your alternatives. Generally in the investment world, to realize greater returns you must undertake greater risks. In the long run this can be counter productive. For a more in-depth discussion on this topic, see the Investment Strategies chapter.

> b) **Reduce your personal spending.** In my view, this is not an effective alternative. When you've been accustomed to a certain lifestyle, it's hard to be satisfied with less. Over the years, I've found using strategies to increase income are much more effective. The excep-

tion relates to tax planning and/or debt reorganization. Poorly organized debt is often a major reason why dental families don't have the Cash Flow available for their long-term Wealth Creation needs. Thankfully, even little changes in the way your debts are structured can work wonders on your cash flow. We'll look at this issue again in a later chapter.

c) **Change your transition objectives.** The more money you want to live on after transition, the greater the sum you'll have to accumulate. The closer you are to your transition objective, the more aggressive your Wealth Creation strategies will have to be to build up identified shortfalls in required retirement capital. Or you can always decide to change these parameters in your goals. Specifically, you could decide to live on less in retirement and/or do your transition later than originally planned. Both of these changes have the potential of bringing your objectives into line with your resources, or of bridging what I refer to as the Resource Gap.

Other Transition considerations

What follows are a number of transition considerations you may want to address, depending on your circumstances.

Investments in equipment

If you're 7 to 10 years from transition, should you be making any investments in equipment or leaseholds that will facilitate the marketability of your practice? If equipment needs to be replaced prior to your transition, talk to the practice valuator on your team. Many dentists wait to spruce up their office and replace old equipment until just prior to their full transition. In effect, they're "getting the practice ready for sale". While this can help facilitate a faster sale, it's not always a good financial decision. Depending on the useful life of the asset involved, you may want to consider investing earlier rather than later.

Staff

Talk to the legal member of your advisory team well in advance of your transition date. You want to be sure you understand how to handle your duties and obligations as an employer.

Make sure your agreements are in good shape.

Do you have an associate? If so, a well-structured agreement is critical. No purchaser is going to pay top dollar for your practice when there's the possibility that an associate could move out and take patients. Of course, everyone recognizes the limitations on enforcing such agreements these days. However, it's always better to have a good agreement in place, prepared by a lawyer familiar with the practice of dentistry and the appropriate case law.

Do you have a cost sharing arrangement in place? Are you in a partnership. A common problem I see with these types of agreements that can affect transition planning is the first right of refusal wording. The majority of these agreements I review require that the cost sharing associate or partner who wishes to sell first offer the other party to the arrangement his or her practice for sale.

If the other parties to the agreement refuse to buy, the wording in these agreements doesn't leave you free to easily seek another buyer. Why? Because any change in the final price or terms typically requires the vendor to go back to their cost-sharing associate/s or partner/s and again offer them the right to buy. Generally this must be done in writing and you typically must provide them with a period of time, say 30 days, to make up their mind and get back to you. In principle, this doesn't sound too bad. But practically speaking, it can present a problem. It can cost a lot for a potential buyer to do all the due diligence necessary to make an investment in your practice. Purchasers may be reluctant to negotiate for a practice and spend the money on lawyers, accountants, and so on if there's a chance the vendor's cost-sharing associate/s or partner/s will exercise their right of first refusal. In addition, purchasers may not want to waste time waiting around for that period of time your cost-sharing associate/s or partner/s have to make up their mind.

My recommendation is that you have your agreements modified to provide all parties with greater flexibility. The agreement could state that the vendor has to get a professional valuation that is representative of Fair Market Value (FMV). The practice should then be offered to the vendor's cost sharing associates or partners for that FMV price. If they decide not to buy after a reasonable period of time, say 30 to 60 days, then they should sign off and leave you free to sell your practice to whomever you choose. In this case, one of the concerns many groups have is, what if you sell to someone the other parties to the arrangement don't like or can't get along with on a professional level? To offer some comfort, the agreement can provide that the person you sell to must be qualified and have a good reputation. Your lawyer should be able to help you with the appropriate wording. Just explain what you would like in plain language. It will be his or her job to turn what you say into suitable 'legalese'.

Investment strategies

Your investment strategies should be designed to maintain the integrity of your capital and grow in accordance with the assumptions you used regarding their growth. An important point to remember is that when it comes to investments, no one knows what the future will bring. The only aspect about investing that you can control with any certainty is risk. (See Investment Strategies chapter.)

Tax planning

It's vital that you have the proper tax planning in place. This book contains a chapter on Tax Planning that covers alternatives that have been employed successfully by other dentists. The idea of the Tax Planning chapter is not to make you a tax expert. Rather, this information should allow you to have meaningful discussions with the financial members of your transition advisory team. There's no point in paying extra tax if you don't have to, provided that your tax strategies aren't too extreme. Stick to proven, mainstream strategies, and stay away from tax-sheltered investment and insurance products unless they've been thoroughly reviewed by a fee-for-service expert, who has no conflicts of interest.

Monitoring your progress

I recommend that you monitor your progress regularly and update your transition strategies at least every 12 months. Ideally, consider quarterly reviews for monitoring purposes. At the end of each quarter, simply set aside a little time to do your review. You'll want to know if the practice (production, expenses and profitability) is performing according to expectations, if your spending is in line with your assumptions, and if your investment portfolio is producing the results you require.

At the end of the year, review what has happened over the previous 12-month period with your advisory team, and consider what might be reasonably expected to change over the next 12 months. Typical changes include:

- an increase in your fee guide
- a staff change, particularly a producer like a hygienist or an important position such as a receptionist
- regulatory changes, such as a change in tax legislation
- the economic or investment outlook
- your transition goals
- your personal circumstances and/or needs

A review of actual performance and consideration of changes that will occur in the next 12-month period will help you put a meaningful new plan in place for the coming year

The non-financial implications of your transition

The non-financial implications of your transition were dealt with in considerable detail in Chapter I, STEP 10, but its importance bears some repetition. Moving from a busy dental practice to retirement is more than the successful disposition of a practice and financial stability. It's a question of "What is going to bring fulfillment for the rest of your life?" My experience has been that the most successful retired dentists are those who planned with the same good sense and enthusiastic approach they used to build their dental career. They had a goal and a plan to participate in some meaningful activity that happily contributes to using up a good deal of the 2000 extra hours a year now at their disposal. After all, I've been told more than once that you can only play so much golf, travel or sit in the sun before life becomes a dull routine.

The next three chapters deal specifically with:
- Wealth Management Strategies
- Wealth Creation Strategies (where your assessments indicate that you do have the discretionary cash flow to build the required wealth)
- Wealth Creation where there is an identified Resource Gap

You may find it interesting to read each of these chapters in detail. Or, in the interest of time, you may want to review in depth only the chapter that specifically applies to your unique situation.

CHAPTER FIVE

TRANSITION STRATEGIES

PART TWO: WEALTH MANAGEMENT STRATEGIES

This chapter will help those who:

- Do have sufficient investable assets for relative financial security

- have a good understanding of their Current Position

- have clearly defined and properly quantified long term retirement goals

If you've determined that you have the required capital today, or have an asset base that if left invested until your transition could grow to the level needed for your relative financial security – congratulations! That's quite an accomplishment in today's world, and it must be satisfying to recognize that you're in such a good fiscal position. The principal focus of transition and retirement strategies for you can be summed up with the term Wealth Management. To maintain this desirable financial position will take effort.

BARRY'S COACHING ADVICE

 Have your Current Position calculations and projections checked and double-checked by the financial members of your transition advisory team!

It's important that you ensure no errors were made in arriving at the figures for your Current Position. It's also critical to ensure that the assumptions used by you and your team were reasonable. Let me refer to a case from our files to illustrate the importance of this point.

CASE STUDY

A new client came into our office a number of years ago, who, in addition to his practice, also had an outside investment in another business. This was a relatively new business that appeared to have great potential. At the time, he was approximately eight years away from his intended transition date. In discussing his Current Position, he felt strongly about the future value of this outside company. The assumptions he used for the growth of this asset over the next eight years and his expectations with respect to selling the company someday were extremely aggressive. My client's role in this new venture was to supply investment capital. He wasn't actively involved in the day-to-day running of the company.

The question that immediately came to mind was, is it reasonable to use aggressive assumptions about this operating company in planning for his transition, or not? Statistics show that the success rates of new ventures aren't good. At first, every start up has a rosy outlook but unfortunately, a high percentage of them aren't even in existence after ten years.

As it happened, using very aggressive assumptions about the success of this company indicated that this client would have virtually no need for any additional savings to meet his transition goals. On the other hand, the success of the plan was heavily dependent on the success of this one asset. When we removed it from the equation there was a significant shortfall between what would be needed upon retirement and expected growth of his other assets. My advice was to proceed with a Wealth Creation plan designed to build the required capital for his transition goals for the first few years.

There are just too many unknowns associated with new companies to have such an important issue as your transition heavily dependent on its successful outcome. In this case, if the investment in the company didn't work out, there wouldn't be a problem. If the company does turn out to be a success, it would be a bonus and we could make adjustments to our figures.

BARRY'S COACHING ADVICE

 As a general guideline, when it comes to assumptions err on the conservative side.

There's a form of analysis called Probability Analysis that you may find useful in determining how realistic your assumptions are. The idea is to vary assumptions, such as inflation rates, investment returns, taxation, and other key factors to measure the probability of the projected outcome turning out as anticipated. Ask a financial member of your transition team to perform this type of analysis, particularly if you're within a few years of your intended full transition date. It will help to provide you with confidence in your strategies. Incidentally, there are computer programs available – your advisor will likely have one – that can facilitate such analysis.

Are you making assumptions about the sale of your practice?

If your planning relies on selling the practice for a specific amount, and if you have not already done so, get a valuation from a creditable practice valuator (who should be considered part of your transition advisory team). Assuming your valuation confirms the value you have used in your analysis, the focus between now and your transition date, as it relates to the practice, must be on managing its value to achieve that end.

To help you do this, you may want to take advantage of the update programs many practice brokers and valuators offer. If you've been thinking about slowing down as you get closer to your transition date, check with your valuator first to make sure you fully understand the impact this decision could have on the potential resale value of the practice.

Tax planning is another reason to invest in a professional valuation. Many practitioners who count on the sale of the practice to help fund their transition goals, often don't have a good idea of the tax implications of the final sale. A professional practice valuation will allocate goodwill, equipment, leaseholds, and supplies. This is vital information that the financial members of your advisory team will need. A review of planning alternatives when selling the practice can be seen in the tax planning section in the chapter on Tax Strategies for Transition and Beyond.

In estimating the impact of the potential sale on your transition planning, you may want to consider some other value management activities, such as:

Would you like to try one of the partial transition variations?

This is an option well worth considering for practitioners who have the required financial resources today to sufficiently meet their transition vision. Of course, everyone has heard about the many associate arrangements that end badly. While there are no guarantees, there are steps you can take that can help to improve the odds of a favourable outcome. Typically in a partial transition, a potential purchaser of a portion of your practice is brought into the office as an associate for a specified period of time. If everything works out after a suitable trial period, he or she "buys in". This could mean they simply buy charts from you, or they buy charts and a share of the office as a cost-sharing colleague, or they form a partnership.

You'll have a greater chance of a successful outcome if you and your advisory team work out your preferences and all specifics in advance of the associate joining your practice. This includes:

- First review your practice to make sure you have the net new patient flow (new patients less patients leaving the practice) to keep the associate busy and allow him or her to achieve their production potential. A well thought out plan, including a marketing program, to integrate the associate into the practice has proven to be a key factor in successful associate arrangement outcomes.
- Consider what you want in an associate and potential partner or cost-sharing colleague.
- Consider involving your staff to help define an ideal candidate.
- Prepare a written profile of the ideal candidate. Having a written profile will help you compare specific candidates to your ideal.

- Have a valuation prepared to determine the price in advance.
- Decide how long the probation period will be (typically six months to a year) and what will happen if he or she doesn't "buy in".
- Work out details such as what rooms the associate can use, what staff will be assigned and what you expect from him or her in relation to hours, production, etc.

In fact, you would be well advised to have an agreement prepared in advance by a lawyer who understands dental practices. I also recommend that you do a Kolbe test to provide you with information on your strengths and weaknesses and among other things, with whom you might best work. Then have any potential associate also do one, and compare their results with your own. Kolbe tests are useful to determine whether an associate candidate's personality is likely to complement your own. They aren't costly, and can be accessed with a credit card through the Internet, at www.kolbe.com. Meyers Briggs and Insight also offer similar types of tests, which can be useful in determining a potential associate's compatibility with yourself and your team.

BARRY'S COACHING ADVICE

 I recommend that one of your key criteria for selecting a candidate be communication skills. Dentists who are good communicators are often more readily accepted by staff and patients, and ultimately more productive.

CHAPTER SIX

TRANSITION STRATEGIES

PART THREE: WEALTH CREATION STRATEGIES

This chapter will help those who:

- have a good understanding of their Current Position

- have clearly defined and properly quantified long-term retirement goals

- **Don't** currently have enough net free investment capital to meet retirement goals, but **do** have discretionary cash flow available to set aside funds identified as the amount necessary to build the required pool of retirement capital

After assessing what your financial situation is today (your Current Position) relative to your clearly defined goals, you'll fall into one of the three categories covered in the introduction to Transition Strategies in Chapter 4. What follows in this chapter is appropriate for those whose situation is best described by the second category:

You do not have enough net free capital, if invested today, to expect that it would grow to a level sufficient to finance your retirement.

However, your analysis indicates that you do have the uncommitted Cash Flow to meet the identified savings need.

I call this uncommitted cash flow Discretionary Cash. Discretionary Cash represents after-tax income that you don't need to finance your lifestyle. At this point you may be asking, "If I have all this cash left over each year, where did it go?" Well, unless you have some system in place to manage it, this cash tends to be spent on secondary priorities or on impulse. When you look back it's almost like the cash evaporated, because when money is spent in this manner it's hard to remember where it went.

Discretionary Cash Flow is one of the most valuable financial resources you have. It can have a powerful impact on your financial security, level of financial stress, and freedom to live your life the way you want. Knowing this, I have experimented with various systems over the years to find the best one to effectively harness this potent resource. The end result is a system I call Banking By Objectives (BBO). It's easy to set up, simple to work with, and successful if followed.

The BBO system was explained in Chapter Two. In my experience, BBO is a very effective way to manage your cash flow and focus your discretionary cash resources on your most important objectives. In fact, I use it myself.

A quick note on using automatic BBO systems

Many dental practices have operating lines of credit, and there's nothing wrong with having one. Few businesses operate efficiently without borrowed funds. Typically, a line of credit operates as follows: deposits automatically decrease the amount owing, and withdrawals (writing a cheque) increase it. If you have an operating line of credit in your practice, it's important to make sure that the savings aren't coming from an increase in the amount owing under the practice liability.

If you have a line of credit that's generally used within the practice, I recommend that you do the transfers involved yourself. An Internet banking capability is perfect in these circumstances. If your assumptions are correct and you have the discretionary funds to meet your identified savings objective, there should be no increase in your debt obligations as a result of the BBO program!

On the other hand, if you find that the amount owing on your line of credit increases beyond normal use levels after setting up the BBO system, you may not have the discretionary cash you thought you did. In this case, you would want to review the reasons for the increase with the financial member of your transition advisory team. It may even be necessary to switch your strategies to the ones referred to in Chapter 7, Wealth Creation – the Resource Gap.

CASE STUDY

Dr. J and his wife, M, live and practice in a major urban centre. Dr. J purchased the practice approximately 22 years ago. He just turned 50 while M is age 46. Both are in good health. They have one son who is at university in his second year of an arts program, and another son who has not yet finished high school. Their second son, at this point, doesn't appear to be interested in going on to university. They feel he will likely attend the local community college.

Their goals are to educate their children, and for J to do a full transition in 10 years at age 60. All in all, Dr. J and his wife feel that they could finance a satisfying retirement lifestyle on what $75,000 after-tax would buy today.

Now let's use Dr. J's situation to look at some numbers. Dr. J's Current Position at the time that we first established his transition plan looked like the following:

Practice	
Practice Gross	$780,000
Practice Expenses	$452,400
Salary to M	$ 42,000
Net Practice Income	$285,600
Personal Income	
Dr. J	$285,600
M	$ 42,000
Net Inflow of Funds	$327,600
Expenditures	
Income Tax (avg rate = 36%)	$117,936
Personal Living Expense Estimate	$ 90,000
Principal on Practice Debt	$ 22,000

Debt Service on Cottage Mortgage	$ 6,395
University Costs for son	$ 15,000
RRSPs	$ 21,600
Total Expenditures	**$272,931**
Surplus/Shortfall	**$ 54,669**

Net Worth

Assets

Cash or near cash	$ 22,000
Practice valuation (after tax)	$350,000
RRSPs	$575,000
Non-Registered Investments	$ 85,000
RESPs	$ 65,000
House	$450,000
Cottage	$170,000
Cars	$ 45,000
Household Effects	$120,000
Total Assets	**$1,882,000**

Liabilities

Practice Line of Credit	$ 40,000
Practice Renovation Loan	$180,000
Cottage Mortgage	$ 48,000
Total Liabilities	**$268,000**
Net Worth	**$1,614,000**

Net assets that could currently be devoted towards retirement income are:

- The practice less an allowance for selling and legal costs of, say $40,000, and practice debt of $220,000 for a net of $90,000

- RRSPs of $575,000
- The non-registered portfolio of $85,000
- Therefore net assets total $750,000

Working with the financial members of their advisory team, Dr. J and M have determined they have a savings need, in addition to regular RRSP contributions, of $46,999 or $3,916.58 per month.

Dr. J and his wife, according to the assessment of their current position, have discretionary cash of $54,669 or $4,555.75 per month. Generally, this objective should be realistically attainable. In fact, that was the case in the actual situation from our files. There is one other benefit that is worth noting. Dr. J and his wife should have a surplus after their savings figure of $7,670. That's about $640 per month. Knowing this figure has helped them manage their income and expenses because they understand how much they can afford to spend on secondary priorities or impulse items.

Their BBO system was set up on a priority basis as follows:

First: Personal Living Account (with overdraft protection)

Two deposits of $3,750 each were made from the practice account each month, one on the first of the month and the other on the 15th. At the end of each month an additional deposit of $532.92 was made to this account for payment of the cottage mortgage. From this account, all other personal expenses were paid, including credit card payments.

Second: The Tax Account

Assuming funds were available at the end of the month, a deposit was made of the sum needed to make the required quarterly tax remittance on the 15th. In this case, we only have to be concerned about Dr. J's income tax because his wife's tax is remitted through source deductions. The amount to be deposited was $8,500 a month.

Third: The Education Funding Account

While their education costs are estimated to be $15,000 annually, the monthly demand for money can fluctuate greatly. Dr. J deposited $1,250 per month to track these costs. However, when tuition has to be paid or books purchased (not to mention those calls from their son explaining all the excellent and logical reasons why his living allowance did not last!), they sometimes have to pre-fund this account. When that happens, the funds come from their cash reserve, net discretionary cash after savings for financial independence, or if necessary, from a personal line of credit they have for such emergencies. From that point, all available funds that would have accumulated from the $1,250 per month deposits are used to repay the funds taken from their cash reserves or the line of credit.

Fourth: The Financial Independence Savings Account

Dr. J and his wife decided to deposit a rounded savings amount of $4,000 into this account. Each quarter, provided the funds are not needed for an emergency, a decision is made as to how to invest these accumulated savings ($16,000) as part of their long term investment strategy (see chapter on Investment Strategies).

Fifth: The RRSP Account

Dr. J and his wife set aside, provided the funds are available, $1,800 per month so that they will have the necessary cash when it comes time to make their annual RRSP contribution. They know they get the best returns from their RRSPs by making their deposits earlier, say at the beginning of the year rather than the following February for the year that has just past. These deposits therefore, fund an advance contribution to the RRSP each year.

Last but not least: Discretionary Spending Account

The remaining discretionary cash estimate of $555 per month is deposited to this account when it's available. Note that the principal payments on the practice debt are paid through the practice accounts.

Monitoring your BBO system

Monitoring your system is important because assumptions don't always work as expected. Things like tax laws, inflation, actual investment returns (or heaven forbid, investment losses) and so on, will impact your objective. One of the great things about the BBO money management system is that it facilitates monitoring. It's really a great feedback system without all the hassles of a paper or computer budget. A simple review of your various bank accounts will tell you whether you're 'on plan' or not.

If everything is working properly, you'll be able to see your results and experience the satisfaction that comes with being in control of your finances. On the other, if at the end of a particular fiscal quarter the BBO system hasn't worked as anticipated, you can make modifications in a timely manner.

What if the program is not working as planned? We all know that the inflows and outflows of cash from the practice sometimes fluctuate quite dramatically. Some months are shorter than others, you take holidays, and sometimes you can have a great month because of extra comprehensive cases. That's why deposits to the BBO must be prioritized. In any given month when there is not enough cash available to make all the planned deposits, the funds that are available must be used for the most important purpose. Over the course of any given quarter, the averages should generally equal your plan.

BARRY'S COACHING ADVICE

Although rare, it can happen that your cash flow turns out to be higher than expected. In this case, you would see either your operating line of credit decrease or a build up of funds in your practice account. I recommend that these funds be set aside but not touched until you are sure they are not going to be needed.

When the BBO system doesn't work, it's due to one of three reasons:

First: It's possible there was a human error, either on your part or as often occurs, on the part of the bank.

Second: Your inflow of cash was lower than anticipated.

Third: Your outflow in terms of practice or personal expenditures was higher than anticipated.

Depending on the reasons as noted above, you may have to adapt your savings plan for the year. It's important to consider whether or not the money will be available to make up the deficit by the end of the year. If the answer is No, the best advice is to go back to the proverbial drawing board and do some recalculating.

Updating your BBO

At the end of 12 months, it's time to create a new savings plan for the coming year. This review process helps to ensure that your planning and strategies remain current and meaningful. Timing is important. Establish well in advance the time to do this update with the appropriate members of your advisory team, and make sure this time commitment is noted in your office schedule. To make sure you're all working on the same schedule, the steps are as follows:

Establish a new current position.

1. Quantify your goals again, taking into account your progress over the last year and the fact you're now one year older.

2. Work out what the new savings figure needs to be, given the results you had in the past year, combined with your outlook for the coming year.

Repeating this process every year will help you to adjust to changes that may affect your financial security, such as inflation, tax regulation, practice income, investment returns, and the economic outlook.

In summary, it's my hope that this extensive case study shows that the best way to capture the required portion of discretionary cash is to put in place a system that's easy to work with and simple to monitor.

CHAPTER SEVEN

TRANSITION STRATEGIES

PART FOUR: HOW TO DEAL WITH A RESOURCE GAP

This chapter will help those who:

- do have a Resource Gap, meaning that they don't have the current resources or the required discretionary cash to meet their goals

- have a good understanding of their Current Position

- have clearly defined and properly quantified long-term retirement goals

It's said that understanding you have a problem is the first step in solving it. The knowledge that you have a Resource Gap can empower you to take action that will provide control of your financial affairs. By doing so now, you won't have nasty surprises down the road, and you can build toward the future that's right for you and your family. So let's get started! There are fundamentally three options you can choose from to deal with your Resource Gap:

Option 1: Increase your inflow

Option 2: Decrease your outflow

Option 3: Change your goals

Option 1: Increase your inflow

When facing a Resource Gap, many clients determine that increasing inflow is by far the most preferable of the three options. Inflow is the net Cash Flow available from your practice after tax. For many practitioners, that means increasing gross production. If that is your preferred alternative, it will be critical to properly define just how much of an increase you will need.

Let's consider a Resource Gap example. With the help of your transition advisory team you have determined it necessary to set aside $35,000 per year, in addition to your RRSP contributions, to reach your transition goals. Suppose it's apparent from your Current Position that at this point in time you only have $15,000 of discretionary cash available. The net result is a Resource Gap of $20,000, after-tax.

Think of this process as a bottom-up exercise. Unfortunately, the actual figure you need to obtain is not $20,000. Why? Because to that $20,000 you must first add tax. If you're earning the money personally from an unincorporated practice, this additional money will most likely be coming in, for tax purposes, at the top marginal tax rate. In Ontario, the top rate in 2003 was approximately 46%. (In this example I have used a 2003 tax rate from only one province. To be meaningful, you will have to adapt the example to the province where you live and the year the calculation was prepared.) For the purpose of this exercise, let us assume that about 54 cents out of every extra dollar you make can be identified with your Resource Gap. If you take your objective of $20,000 and divide it by 54%, the answer is the pre-tax incremental amount of $37,037 ($20,000/.54) that you need to bring into income. But you're not there yet. This figure, to be of value in a strategic planning sense, still needs greater definition. You must also answer the question of how much additional variable overhead you'll have to incur to generate this incremental pre-tax income.

Variable overheads or expenses

Variable overheads or expenses are an important consideration when you're trying to identify what additional income must be brought in to reach your objectives. These are the expenses that increase or decrease with the ebb and flow of practice volume. When identifying the target amount that you need to earn, ask yourself what you'll have to spend to generate this additional revenue. An obvious example is supplies. Assume that historically, supplies represent 7% of your gross revenue; therefore, when you bill $1.00, seven cents of that dollar can be expected to go to supplies. Here's a list of less obvious variable expenses to consider as well:

- Will your staff costs go up?
- Do you need to hire an associate to handle the drill and fill work so you can do more comprehensive work that will increase your hourly production?
- Will funds have to be spent on advertising or promotion?
- Will there be additional equipment costs?

You may simply know off the top of your head what expenses are variable. If you don't, or if you need a reference source to make sure you've identified all variable expenses, I'd recommend looking at your Profit and Loss statements (sometimes referred to as Income Statements). Typically your accountant, as part of your annual financial statements, prepares Profit and Loss statements. They're the best source for information like this. Simply assemble statements that cover a few years. Calculate the percentages that each expense item represents of that year's gross revenue. Identifying what expenses increased or decreased (other than normal inflationary increments) with a corresponding increase or decrease in that gross revenue number will help you identify all your variable costs.

For purposes of our example, assume that your variable costs work out to be 20 per cent. In other words, out of every dollar of extra revenue (up to a point), 80 cents should drop to your bottom line. Going back to the pre-tax figure we worked out to arrive at an after tax sum of $20,000, divide $37,037 by 80% ($37,037/.80). According to my calculations, that would be $46,296.25.

BARRY'S COACHING ADVICE

 It's always prudent to plan for contingencies, so round off your objective amount to the next highest $10,000. In this case, we are talking about $50,000 of additional practice production to produce that $20,000 needed to make up the Resource Gap.

Any annual figure that you calculate is likely to be a big number (such as the $50,000 in the above example). It may be a little intimidating. The secret is to break down such large sums into workable bites. For example, assume you work 230 days per year. If we go back to our figure of $50,000 and divide it by 230, you would only have to earn an additional $217.39 per day in incremental production to meet your objective. When you think in terms of $50,000, it's difficult to come up with workable strategies for such a big number. It's a lot easier to deal with a number such as $218.

After properly defining what you would need to produce to sufficiently increase your inflow, the next question you must answer is, can it be done and how? There's a basic rule when it comes to establishing strategies. They should be realistically attainable. Can you develop strategies to bring in an additional $218 per day? For many practitioners it can be as simple as giving their receptionist specific directions on how to book their day. Have her book your schedule to meet the required daily objective, not just fill holes in the schedule. The receptionist may even find it motivating because at the end of the day she'll be able to experience a sense of accomplishment if the objective is met. Of course if the objective is not met both of you will know, presenting you with the opportunity to work together to take remedial action.

There are many more strategies to consider besides targeted appointment scheduling. To bring in new patients, you may consider getting more community exposure by writing articles, public speaking, sending out a newsletter or networking. Just regularly asking for referrals can help. You may even want to examine the effectiveness of your recall system, or perhaps consider changing your service mix so your hourly rate increases, or offering extended hours.

You will have to decide what alternative or group of alternatives is best for you. Some alternatives will be more complex and expensive than others, so list them all and choose the simplest and least expensive first, unless you're concerned that they won't be effective. You may even want to hire a practice consultant to help you develop your strategies. If so, be very specific about what you want from the consultant's engagement because they can be expensive. Without direction, their strategies can also involve more practice disruption than your circumstances really require. Tell them the exact amount of additional gross revenue you need and remember, to be successful the engagement must also produce enough additional revenue to pay their fee. It's also important to have a monitoring process to keep track of their progress and expenses.

Another strategy for increasing your bottom line

In the preceding paragraphs, I suggested that you assemble several years of Profit and Loss statements. Use them to calculate what percentage each category of expense represents in terms of gross revenue, and then compare these figures to practice or industry averages. Are any of your costs too high? Could they be reduced without affecting the viability of your practice or business?

Comparing your expenses with industry averages such as the Annual Economic Survey the Ontario Dental Association publishes(most associations have this information available) helps identify expenses in your practice that may be unusually high and therefore warrant attention. If it appears your expenses are abnormally high relative to the profession as a whole, discuss strategies for reducing them with your transition advisory team. It very often can be worth the exercise.

I recall working with a practitioner whose practice had slowed down a little. The problem was that his gross revenue also slowed down but his fixed expenses didn't change. As a result, his personal income was drastically reduced. The solution was to move another practitioner into his office to share space and fixed expenses. This was done together with a change in calendar management so that my client hardly ever saw his cost-sharing colleague. Both practices enjoyed a significant increase to their bottom line. While opportunities to decrease fixed practice expenses are not always easy to identify, the possibility shouldn't be ignored.

Before I finish this section, I want to comment on partnerships. If you're in a full partnership, it can be difficult to increase your individual income. Typically, partners take a portion of their personal production and the rest goes into a common account to pay expenses, after which the remainder is split among all partners. Some partnerships don't allow the partners to take a portion of their individual production, but instead everything is channeled into the common pot after expenses are paid and then the profits are divided. In circumstances such as this, if you worked harder to earn additional income, your partners may be sincerely grateful.

In a partnership, either all partners agree that they'll work to increase the bottom line or you may need to find another way to earn the additional required revenue. It may mean restructuring your agreements, which can be a difficult task. If you aren't able to increase income, you may be forced to move on to the other two options – decreasing your outflow or changing your goals.

BARRY'S COACHING ADVICE

Set up a system such as Banking By Objectives (Chapter 2) to make sure funds are available for their intended purpose. It's all too easy when funds are mixed in the general pool of family monies to make an impulse decision to expend these additional resources. Set the money aside first to fund your transition and other important priorities, and then you can spend the rest.

Option 2: Decrease your outflow

By way of general comment, let me say that in over 20 plus years of working with dentists, I have found that the least effective alternative when dealing with a Resource Gap is to decrease personal lifestyle expenses. It just doesn't seem to work – and many times it causes strife within the family. Only in extreme cases, where no other alternatives exist, do I recommend reducing personal expenditures. That being the case, let's look at some ways that can be effective at reducing outflow.

Reorganizing debt

No one likes debt, and that means people are often committed to amortization schedules that are too rapid. The argument tends to go, "I'll pay off my debts, and then I'll save for retirement". The problem with this is that people lose one of the great benefits of investing: the power of compounding. Now, I'm not suggesting that you shouldn't pay off your debts. Rather, it's one place to look if you're trying to find the funds to meet a defined savings objective.

Some actions to consider are:
- consolidating loans
- taking a longer amortization period
- arranging for deductible debts to be interest only, so that all the principal can be applied to non-deductible debt

If you have a great deal of practice debt, consider professional incorporation and paying it back from the corporate entity. While the interest on practice debt is tax deductible, repayment of the principal is not. For example, if we assume for ease of calculation that the top marginal tax rate is 50%, paying back $1.00 of principal on your practice debt takes $2.00 of pre-tax income.

Professional Corporations, on the other hand, generally qualify for the small business deduction. That means the corporation's tax rate (see Tax Planning chapter for more information) is much lower and there is more after-tax money to pay back the principal on the practice loan. For example, assume the corporation has a tax rate of 20%. Rather than having to earn $2.00 pre-tax to pay back $1.00 of debt as mentioned earlier, you would only have to earn $1.20. That's a significant advantage! Be sure to discuss this alternative in detail with your transition advisory team. Professional incorporation is not for everyone and it can be expensive.

Selling redundant assets

I once had a client who had a beautiful cottage that was worth a significant amount of money. Not only did it cost a great deal in terms of maintenance, property taxes, and operating costs, it also had a non-deductible mortgage. The client was forced to make a decision. Did he and his spouse prefer to keep the cottage, in which case projections indicated he wouldn't be able to do a transition until his mid-sixties, or did they think it was more important to be in a position to do a full transition by his late fifties? Decisions like this are always difficult. What it comes down to is prioritizing what's truly important to you. In the case mentioned above, the client decided to keep the cottage and change his transition goal.

Reducing income tax

This can be very complex. In Chapter 8 I've outlined a number of tax strategies that are common in dental practices and other businesses. These strategies include:

- a discussion on Professional Incorporation
- Hygiene and Technical Services Companies
- Retirement Compensation Arrangements
- other strategies helpful in reducing taxes payable in a given year and therefore your outflow

Once again, discuss these strategy options in detail with your transition advisory team to make sure they are appropriate for your circumstances.

Budgeting versus using a Priority Spending System

If you decide to reduce your personal lifestyle expenditures, I'd recommend you work on a Priority Spending format. This system works on a monthly basis where spending is related to net cash flow generated by the practice in the previous month. It has to be the previous month because you make spending decisions in real time, but typically you don't have information on what's happening with income and expenses and the resulting available cash on a daily basis. The answer is to operate with a line of credit in the practice and restrict your draws to what cash was available from the previous month so that you don't overspend.

With these funds, the first category of expenses that should be paid includes basic living expenses, such as food, insurance, shelter, clothing and transportation. Basic living expenses do not include any extras like entertainment, or any form of discretionary spending. Basic in this case, really means basic. Next, taxes and debt service, if any, are to be paid. So far, these are costs that you really must pay. But from this point on, you have decisions to make.

Reducing your personal expenditures is all about trade-offs. What's your most important priority? If your priority is creating financial security for yourself that will allow you to achieve your long-term transition goals, then the next item that should be set aside is the sum you've identified as your savings objective. Once again, set these monies aside in a separate account so that they're identified with their purpose. Any money left over after these expenses and priorities have been taken care of can then be spent.

Option 3: Change your goals

If you can't increase inflow, and if, after examining the various trade-offs involved with decreasing outflow you decide this also isn't a good option, you must look at changing your objective. The sooner you do this, the better. There are two general changes you can make that should have a dramatic impact on the Resource Gap you have identified:

1. You can decide to retire later. This means you will have longer to accumulate the necessary resources and you will be living off your assets (as opposed to your earnings) for less time.
2. You can plan on spending less when you retire.

If, after completing a full transition, you plan to live on $150,000 per year after-tax, it would take substantially more retirement capital than living on $75,000 per year after-tax. When working with your transition team's financial members, don't forget that at some point you may have the option of reducing retirement spending and at the same time, allowing your accumulated capital to grow. In general, most people don't spend the same way at age 80 that they did at age 60. One important consideration to keep in mind however, is that it costs a significant amount of money if there is a need in later years for assisted living or a retirement residence.

Time is of the essence

Successfully dealing with a Resource Gap is possible. It just requires looking carefully at your priorities and your lifestyle. The important thing is to act now – even with the smallest step. The sooner you put measures in place to close up your Resource Gap, the sooner you'll feel better about your overall transition plans.

CHAPTER EIGHT

DEVELOP TAX STRATEGIES FOR TRANSITION AND BEYOND

This chapter will help you:

- Know your pre-transition tax planning options

- Understand the various strategies available for reducing tax when you sell your practice

- Be aware of what you can do to implement post-transition tax strategies

Taxation is a vast and complicated topic. For that reason, this chapter will focus only on issues that affect tax planning for your transition. The intent is to give you a better understanding of the tax strategies available which will allow you greater input when working with the financial members of your transition advisory team. This is your future. Knowing what questions to ask can help you feel confident that you've left no "tax stone" unturned.

Specifically, we'll look at strategies in use today that may help you reduce the income tax burden you could face in three specific situations: during pre-transition, when you sell your practice, and during post-transition. By the way, tax planning shouldn't be limited to these stages of your life. Some experts call it a cradle to beyond the grave process, and I agree.

A quick caveat before we begin

Prior to implementing any tax strategy mentioned in this book, you should check with the appropriate members of your transition advisory team (accountant, financial planner/retirement planner) to make sure it's appropriate for your circumstances and complies with Canada Customs and Revenue Agency (CCRA) requirements, interpretations, and practices. Checking with these professionals will also help to ensure that important details and procedures aren't overlooked. Due to the constraints of space, the material provided here is in summary form only.

Overcoming the tax intimidation factor

Albert Einstein once said, "The hardest thing to understand in the world is income tax". Many people feel the same way. Just take a look at the Canadian Tax Act. On one hand, it's contained in a book the size of a very large novel or biography. On the other hand, the wording can be so difficult and vague that its published interpretations, precedents and practices take up what amounts to a fair-sized library!

The good news is that you don't need to have an in-depth knowledge of taxation to come out ahead at tax time. You simply need a qualified team of advisors, who can explain your options well enough to allow you to assess the advice and act on it. If your taxes are planned properly, there are literally tens of thousands and even hundreds of thousands of dollars that can be saved over a lifetime. This brings up another important point. Most financial planners and accountants are good tax generalists. Don't be afraid to ask for a second opinion from a tax specialist if you think your situation, because of complexity or the amount of money in question, warrants it.

BARRY'S COACHING ADVICE

When it comes to tax planning, encourage your transition advisory team to be creative (while of course maintaining compliance with applicable laws and regulations at all times). Your ability to save tax isn't limited to the alternatives discussed in this book. Good tax planning should complement your present financial circumstances, and enhance the likelihood of accomplishing your long-range fiscal goals.

Strategies to reduce income tax liability generally fall into the following three broad categories:

a) Income splitting

Canadians are subject to a marginal tax rate system, which means that as your income increases so does the tax bite on those incremental dollars. Many thousands of dollars can be saved in tax every year by splitting income that would normally be taxed at the top marginal tax rate with someone in your family who's in a lower tax bracket. If it can be planned, for example, that a husband and wife residing in Newfoundland each earn $50,000 per year as opposed to one of them earning $100,000, the tax savings would be well over $10,000 per year.

b) Tax deferral

Under the Canadian Tax System, deferring tax can also make a great deal of sense. It's another category of commonly employed strategies. Your RRSP is a good example. Tax is deferred on deposits within prescribed limits to your RRSP, and on the money earned in your RRSP, until you take it out or until both you and your spouse have passed away. Incorporation is another method of tax deferral. The trick to getting the maximum benefit out of a tax deferral strategy is not just the initial deferral. It's also about bringing that deferred income back into your hands or the hands of another family member at a lower tax rate than that at which you deferred it.

c) Income planning

Dividends and capital gains have a lower effective tax rate than earned income (salary, bonus or the net from an unincorporated practice) or interest income. For example, there can be a benefit in planning the optimum salary/dividend mix if you're professionally incorporated. Or you could use your RRSPs to hold interest-bearing assets. By simply allocating your interest bearing assets to a no-tax environment like an RRSP or IPP (individual pension plan), you'll benefit from higher annual compounding.

BARRY'S COACHING ADVICE

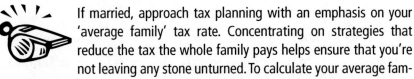 If married, approach tax planning with an emphasis on your 'average family' tax rate. Concentrating on strategies that reduce the tax the whole family pays helps ensure that you're not leaving any stone unturned. To calculate your average family tax rate, take last year's tax returns from each family member and total up all the income. Now total up all the tax that was due on this income. Divide the tax paid by your total family income figure. The answer is your average family tax rate for the period.

SECTION ONE: PRE-TRANSITION TAX PLANNING

This section discusses useful strategies for the period leading up to your transition, that can lower your tax bite, facilitate your savings plan and even contribute to reducing or eliminating your Resource Gap, if you have one.

Income Splitting

Employing a spouse or a child (who is old enough to work) is one of the most commonly used methods of income splitting. When it comes to earned income (salary, for example from the practice) Canada Customs and Revenue Agency (CCRA) takes the position that you should pay someone who's related to you the same as you would pay someone who's not related to you, for the same work. Many practitioners pay their spouses a significant income. The justification for this from CCRA's perspective is that the spouse performs some form of management role in the practice and the greater responsibility justifies the larger salary. If you're going to pay your spouse management wages, I'd recommend you have a job description on file. If you're unsure whether your spouse's compensation package would be considered reasonable, discuss it with the financial members of your advisory team. They can't give you any absolutes or guarantees, but they should have the experience to tell you what's reasonable and what's not.

Many retirement planners recommend that the RRSPs of both spouses should be roughly equal in order to facilitate income splitting upon retirement. This rule of thumb needs additional definition in a dental environment. In most dental families, the practitioner has a much higher income than the spouse. Therefore, the strategy wouldn't be to simply equalize RRSPs, but rather investments in general. If most of the family's investments are in the dentist's name, the resulting investment income could all be subject to the top marginal tax rate.

BARRY'S COACHING ADVICE

 To equalize your holdings between each spouse, you may want to consider having your spouse save his or her salary for investment purposes and using your income to pay for living expenses. If your spouse saves their income for the family's financial security, you should separate funds allocated out of your income for that spouse's personal spending money and other needs. It can be very demeaning for a spouse to ask for money. In my experience financial strategies of this nature work more effectively if both spouses have personal funds they can spend as they see fit.

Other Income Splitting ideas

Attribution Rules prevent you from shifting investment income (dividends and interest) to a spouse or minor child who's in a lower income tax bracket. Under these rules, if you were to loan money at no interest or gift money to your spouse for investment purposes, the resulting dividends or interest would be 'attributed' back to you for tax purposes, thus defeating the strategy. This has resulted in a significant amount of time and creative energy going into designing ways of splitting investment income which won't be caught in the 'attribution net'. Briefly, some of these alternatives are:

a) Incorporation

This is an important pre-transition tax planning strategy. It combines the benefits of income splitting, tax deferral and income planning. In professional practices there are two types of corporations commonly employed: professional corporations (PC) and non-professional or 'normal corporations'. Professional corporations can be quite different from other types of companies, depending on the province where you reside. Some provinces limit ownership of the shares of a PC to a member of the profession. This inhibits income splitting as compared to a normal company. If you reside in such a province, you may want to consider two corporations. One would be a professional corporation where you own the shares, and the other an ordinary company that handles the non-professional components of your practice. These are sometimes referred to as Technical Services Companies or Hygiene Companies. Management companies were commonly used at one time but have fallen into disfavour since the GST came into being. The non-professional company would ideally be owned by your spouse or perhaps a trust where your spouse and children are the beneficiaries. If you've been supporting a relative such as an elderly parent, think about making them a beneficiary of the trust that owns shares in your corporation as well.

Professional incorporation is not for everyone. There can be a number of drawbacks to watch for. When it's first set up, you'll find it quite different from operating an unincorporated practice. For accountants and other financial advisors, working with companies like this is quite simple so they may not think it's necessary to provide you with any extra explanation or support. However, if you and your staff have been working in an unincorporated practice for your whole professional career, the change to a corporate structure can be confusing.

BARRY'S COACHING ADVICE

 Have your accountant or bookkeeper explain the differences between an unincorporated and an incorporated practice and walk you and your staff through what changes will have to be addressed.

Set-up costs can also be expensive and there are additional accounting and filing fees that you'll have to take into account. Further, if you have a negative practitioner's account (where practice liabilities are greater than practice assets) as many dentists do, you may have to report a capital gain if you professionally incorporate.

b) The Kiddie Tax

After-tax corporate profits are generally distributed by providing dividends to shareholders. In the past you could split income by having a trust for the benefit of your minor children own shares of your company and pay them dividends. Depending on the amount paid out, these dividends may not have attracted any tax. However, the rules changed a few years ago. Now if dividends are paid in this manner, where the beneficiary is under the age of 18, they'll attract tax at the highest rate. Therefore, it's no longer prudent to split income in this manner. However, once a child turns 18 this strategy starts to be effective again.

c) Capital Gains Trusts

There's no attribution of capital gains for funds loaned to a trust for a minor child or children (not spouses). A trust used in this manner is sometimes referred to as a Capital Gains Trust. The caution here is that most investments that earn capital gains also earn dividends, and only capital gains are exempt from the attribution rules. If the trust earns dividend income by investing the funds you've loaned to it, that income will be attributed back to you for tax purposes. But when that income is attributed to you, as the higher income member of the family, you shouldn't pay any more tax than you would have paid if the dividends came directly into your hands. Another important thing to keep in mind is that capital losses are also not attributed.

d) Investment portfolio

If your investment portfolio is significantly higher than your spouse's and you need to equalize, you can purchase an asset from him or her for its fair market value. When the spouse invests the proceeds, there should be no concern about attribution of the income.

CASE STUDY

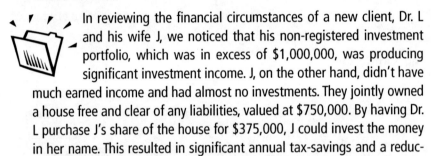 In reviewing the financial circumstances of a new client, Dr. L and his wife J, we noticed that his non-registered investment portfolio, which was in excess of $1,000,000, was producing significant investment income. J, on the other hand, didn't have much earned income and had almost no investments. They jointly owned a house free and clear of any liabilities, valued at $750,000. By having Dr. L purchase J's share of the house for $375,000, J could invest the money in her name. This resulted in significant annual tax-savings and a reduction in the family's average tax rate.

e) Secondary income (for those with a non-registered investment portfolio)

I think this concept is best explained with an example. Suppose you have a large investment portfolio of $500,000 of unregistered assets earning a return of 5%. Of course, any income that it earns will be taxed in your hands. Now let's say you have a trust in place for your minor children who are well under the age of 18. You could loan that $500,000 to the trust. When the trust earned the return of 5%, it would be attributed back to you for tax purposes. That doesn't mean you received it. The money is still in the trust. You just have to pay tax on it.

These earnings are now the property of the trust. If left for five years, the trust would have $ 138,140 capital of its own to invest. At 5%, that means the following year almost $7,000 would be taxed in the hands of your children rather than your hands. In other words, it wouldn't be subject to your high rate of tax. Depending on your circumstances and the age of your children, the resulting tax savings could grow dramatically over the years. Keep in mind that to accomplish this strategy, you should not have to pay any more tax than if you had not taken steps to implement the strategy. By the way, the original capital would be loaned on a demand note basis, so that you as the trustee could simply require the trust to pay it back whenever you wished.

f) Spousal RRSPs

You make the contribution, get the tax deduction, but the asset builds in your spouse's name for use in retirement. What could be easier? Spousal RRSPs are great for setting up income splitting arrangements in retirement.

g) Registered Education Savings Plans

While not contributing directly to your transition plan, RESPs are a good way of splitting income and saving for your children's education, thereby freeing up other resources that can be devoted to your transition plan. There's also the Canada Education Savings Grant, which is 20% of the contribution to a maximum of $400 per annum per child (there is a cumulative maximum per child of $7,200).

Now let's look at Tax Deferral

RRSPs are generally the most commonly used vehicle for tax deferral. The deferral comes when the initial deposit is made, because it's deductible (provided you don't over-contribute) from your taxable income. Deferral also results when the income within the RRSP trust compounds on a tax-free basis. It's important to keep in mind that the maximum benefit comes from making deposits that are deductible at the top marginal rate.

Remember that tax must be paid when funds are eventually withdrawn from the RRSP. Therefore, if your spouse is in a low tax bracket you may want to consider whether or not it makes sense to use up his or her contribution ability at that time. It may be better to have the low-income spouse accumulate such funds outside of the RRSP, even though it may result in some current tax at a low marginal rate. The RRSP carry forward rules allow you to accumulate the ability to make a contribution. In the meantime, you could consider strategies to increase the spouse's income up to the point a deposit to an RRSP would result in a significant deferral.

There's another planning twist that can make good sense in the right circumstances. A low-income spouse can make the RRSP contribution, but choose not to take the deduction in that year. This way the investment grows tax-free, and you can consider strategies to increase taxable income in the future to the point where the deduction can be taken in a year when a significant deferral results.

Retirement Compensation Arrangements

Retirement Compensation Arrangements (RCA) can offer significant income splitting and tax deferral benefits for the unincorporated practice that employs a spouse. It can also be used effectively for you if you're professionally incorporated. Generally, the greatest advantage is realized from this supplemental retirement planning tool when the spouse has worked for the practice for a long time, is over age 50, has earned a significant income from the practice, and doesn't have too much accumulated in RRSPs. But I'm getting ahead of myself.

First let me define a Retirement Compensation Arrangement. It's an arrangement whereby an employer (you, the practitioner or your PC) makes a tax-deductible contribution to a custodian for the benefit of an employee (you or your spouse). In a professional corporation, the company would be the employer and you would be the employee. The custodian sends 50% of the contribution to Canada Customs and Revenue Agency (CCRA) where the money is set aside in a refundable tax account. The other 50% is deposited into an RCA trust for the benefit of the employee (you or your spouse). The money in the trust is then invested.

There are really no rules when it comes to what the trust can invest in, unlike, for example, an RRSP. When the trust earns money on the assets invested within it, 50% of those earnings also go to CCRA where they get added to your RCA refundable tax account. When the employee (you or your spouse) retires and starts to draw income from the RCA trust, CCRA will send $1.00 back from the refundable tax account to the trust for every $2.00 the trust pays out. Sound confusing?

Let's look at a quick example

Suppose the trust paid out $20,000 during the year. CCRA would send $10,000 from the refundable tax account back to the trust. The net effect would be that the funds in the trust went down by $10,000 and the funds in the refundable tax account went down by $10,000. When the trust pays out income to the beneficiary, it's taxable. So if you're required to send money to CCRA for the refundable tax account and then must pay tax when the money is paid out, where's the advantage, you may ask.

Basically, the funds you deposit with the custodian for the RCA should all be deductible at the top marginal rate of tax. When that money is brought back into income, provided proper planning has taken place, it should be subject to a much lower tax rate which results in a net savings.

In the right circumstances, this can be a very powerful planning tool. Fundamentally, you would be making the contributions with funds that would have been, for the most part, going to pay tax anyway, with no chance of that money ever being returned.

Another advantage is that it can be used as a tool to equalize retirement assets between spouses so that the post-transition average family tax rate is kept at a minimum. It can also offer some strategic benefits to those who are doing a full transition early in life – say in their mid to late fifties or even early sixties. In the past we've been able to effectively use income from an RCA to fund living needs without having to draw on RRSPs prior to the beneficiary's age 69. That leaves the money in the RRSP to compound for a longer period of time. RCAs can also be useful in planning around the time you sell your practice, and I'll address this in a moment.

Tax deferral benefits of incorporation

Incorporation offers great deferral benefits if the funds aren't needed for your immediate cash flow and can be left in the company. Corporations have a lower tax rate than you do on income that qualifies for the small business deduction. This is the limit under which qualifying small businesses receive what might be thought of as preferential tax treatment. For provincial tax, this threshold amount varies. Federally, the small business income limits apply to net profits of $250,000 and under (in 2004). This limit is going up at the federal tax level to $300,000 in 2005 and beyond.

Individual Pension Plans (IPP)

An IPP is a registered pension plan that is set up via the corporation for you and/or your spouse (if he or she works for your company). Contribution limits can be significantly higher for an IPP than the maximum RRSP deduction limit. That means a greater deduction and more assets growing tax-free for your retirement. IPPs also offer the added benefit of being protected from creditors.

If you live in a jurisdiction that has permitted professional corporation for some time, you may be able to make what's known as a past service contribution for years of service when you were an employee of your company. Past service contributions can result in significant tax deductions over and above normal contribution levels. Therefore, if you have had a professional corporation in place where you've been employed for a number of years (without a pension plan), it would be worth checking to see if you qualify. A credible actuary should be able to provide you with the answers you need.

BARRY'S COACHING ADVICE

 When it comes time for your transition, it's possible that additional funds could be set aside on a deductible basis in an Individual Pension Plan that would allow you to retire early, have greater spousal benefits, or indexing. This is only possible if you've been an employee of a corporation for a number of years. While they offer many advantages, IPPs aren't for everyone. An IPP can be costly to set up and maintain. Also, it can be more complex to administer. Careful analysis should be done to ensure that an IPP is right for you before proceeding. A combination of RRSPs and RCAs might be a better alternative to consider.

Universal Life Insurance as a tax strategy

Universal Life as an insurance alternative is discussed under Risk Management in Chapter 10. It combines permanent life insurance with the possibility of tax-free growth for the cash that's intended to build up in the policy, within prescribed limits. This cash that builds up in the policy is often referred to as Cash Surrender Value (CSV). Commonly, when promoted as a retirement planning alternative, the strategy involves the policy in combination with a loan from a financial institution.

If you had CSV built up in a universal life policy, and then upon retirement decided to have some of this CSV paid out to support your retirement living needs, the withdrawals would attract some tax. Life insurance is only tax-free when the benefit is paid out upon the death of the insured. The intent of the loan is to avoid such tax while you're alive. There's no income tax on borrowed funds. This strategy is sometimes called an Insured Retirement Plan, and at first glance the concept seems to make a lot of sense.

The savings component or CSV grows tax-free. When you want to use it to help fund your retirement, rather than taking out the CSV and paying the resulting tax, you borrow (within limits) from a financial institution that takes the policy as security. On the death of the insured, proceeds from the life insurance are tax-free. They're first used to pay off the financial institution and the balance goes to your beneficiaries or estate.

Sounds pretty good, doesn't it? However, like so many things, on closer inspection there are some concerns. For example, in many of the proposals I've seen, the assumptions employed are questionable. There are also expensive costs to be factored in, and your money has to be tied up for a long period of time. Therefore, I strongly recommend that an advisor who isn't connected with the sale of the policy carefully analyze any such offerings. The advisor should also have an excellent understanding of your overall needs, what other alternatives are available, and the nuances of such insurance product offerings.

Income Planning

In addition to income splitting and tax deferral, incorporation can offer advantages under this category of tax planning as well as in the areas of practice debt management, other expenses, and the optimum mix of salary and dividends as outlined below.

Practice debt

While the interest on practice debt would normally be deductible, paying back the principal is not. That means that you have to repay any practice debt out of after-tax dollars.

When the corporation pays back principal, it will have more money to do so. For example, if you're in a 46% tax bracket, to repay $100,000 of principal back on a loan, you would have to earn, pre-tax in an unincorporated practice, approximately $185,000. In a corporation with income under the small business deduction threshold mentioned above, assume the tax rate for such profits would be 20%. To repay that same $100,000 from such a corporation, the company would only have to earn $125,000 in after-tax profits. That's a big difference!

Other expenses

While you do get a deduction when buying equipment or leaseholds in the way of the capital cost allowance, this benefit may be over a long period of time. In the meantime, you have had to advance funds for the purchase out of after-tax income. Once again, if it's done through a corporation, there's a lot more money available after-tax. Similarly, it can make a great deal of sense to have your corporation pay for non-deductible expenses that won't result in a taxable benefit to you. Examples are life insurance, and conventions in excess of two per year.

The salary/dividend mix

Dividends from a Canadian corporation receive a tax credit to allow for the fact that the corporation has already paid some tax on that money. Issuing a combination of dividends and salary may result in some tax savings over a salary alone. Keep in mind though, that dividends don't qualify as 'earned income'. You must have some earned income to continue to make RRSP, IPP or even RCA contributions. If you have a corporation, talk to your professional advisor about planning the optimum salary/dividend mix for your circumstances.

BARRY'S COACHING ADVICE

In the pre-transition planning phase of your life, build up a non-registered investment portfolio that isn't in a corporation. In other words, this portfolio would be a pool of tax- paid capital. Once you fully retire, the use of non-registered capital will be important to keep your average family tax rate at a minimum level.

SECTION TWO:

STRATEGIES FOR REDUCING TAX WHEN YOU SELL YOUR PRACTICE

You have a number of alternative strategies to consider for reducing the tax impact on the sale of your practice. In tax planning, a great deal depends on your particular circumstances. Are you incorporated? Does your spouse work for the practice? Are you a member of a partnership? Do you have sizable tax shelter losses? Depending on how you answered those questions, some of the following may be suitable for you:

1. **The structure of many practice purchase agreements make allowances for the spouse of the vendor to provide some consulting to the purchaser for a fee.** The consulting fee will qualify as

earned income for your spouse. This could mean that he or she will have a higher RRSP contribution limit the following year.

2. **If your spouse has been working for you for quite some time, you could pay them a retiring allowance.** An employer can make a tax-deductible payment to a retiring employee in the form of a retiring allowance. The interesting thing about a retiring allowance is that within limits it can be 'rolled' directly into the employee's RRSP without any withholding tax, under special rules relating to such payments. The formula works this way. For years of service prior to 1989, the employee can roll $3,500 per year into his or her RRSP, provided he or she was not a vested member of a pension plan in your office. For years of service from 1989 to 1995, $2,000 per year of service can be 'rolled' tax-free into their RRSP. That's seven years. So if your spouse had worked for you since 1970, you could pay a retiring allowance on the practice sale that is deductible to you and that can be rolled tax-free into their RRSP of $77,000 [(18 yrs x $3,500) + (7 years x $2,000)].

3. **You could make a Retirement Compensation Arrangement (RCA) contribution for your spouse's benefit, if he or she has worked for you for a sufficient length of time.** You could also make an RCA contribution to your own plan if you are an employee of a professional corporation. The only guidelines in the Income Tax Act about how much can be put away into an RCA are that the contributions must be reasonable in the circumstances. My experience with CCRA is that they'll consider a contribution "reasonable in the circumstances" if it's based on a formula relating to the employee's years of service, income, and present RRSP or IPP level. Due to the complexity of the funding formula, have the financial members of your transition advisory team do the calculation, or hire an actuary.

4. **You may be able to sell shares of your professional corporation or your technical services company.** Qualifying shares of Canadian Controlled Private Corporations (which these companies

should be) are eligible for a capital gains exemption. It's often referred to as the Super Exemption. This is part of the Lifetime Capital Gains Exemption (CGE) of $500,000. If you have used the $100,000 that was available up to 1994, then you would only have $400,000 left. Incidentally, if you reside in a province where non-professionals can own shares of a professional corporation, it's possible, in the right circumstances, that both spouses would be able to claim this capital gains exemption – provided that your spouse owned shares of your PC.

While selling shares and sheltering the tax with the CGE may seem like an excellent way to sell your practice free of tax, it's not that simple. While it's great for the vendor, it's not necessarily good for the purchaser. There are no tax deductions by way of depreciation for buying shares, and the purchaser would generally much rather buy the assets of the practice. In this way, they could benefit from the capital cost allowance (depreciation) available on the various asset classes. The moral of the story? If you're incorporated and want to sell the shares to utilize the capital gains exemption, you can expect any interested buyers to negotiate hard to share some of the benefits. Selling shares versus assets will even change the way the valuation is conducted.

BARRY'S COACHING ADVICE

If you're working with a credible practice valuator, ask them what price the shares of your professional corporation might command in the market place versus a more traditional asset sale. Then ask your professional advisors to analyze the pros and cons of this strategy versus the combination of asset sale and other strategies mentioned here. Most importantly, before deciding on this strategy talk to your professional advisors to make sure you don't have Cumulative Net Investment Losses (CNIL). Things like tax-shelter deductions, rental losses and carrying charges create a CNIL balance. A CNIL balance reduces or eliminates your ability to claim the capital gains exemption.

5. **If you have a Professional Corporation (PC) or Technical Service Company (TSC), consider selling assets out of the company rather than the shares.** From the purchaser's point of view, there's no difference between selling assets and buying an unincorporated practice. The benefit for you, the vendor, is the corporation's low rate of tax below the small business deduction levels (as mentioned earlier). In this case, you would enjoy a deferral of the tax until such time as the money is paid out of the PC. For the portion of the goodwill that would represent the other 50% that isn't taxable, the money could be dividended out to you absolutely tax-free. This is due to some special rules relating to what's called a Capital Dividend Account. The balance of the money in the corporation could then be paid out over a period of years, either by way of salary, dividends, or a mix depending on your circumstances. If the sale would create a significant amount of income over the small business deduction threshold, strategies such as a retiring allowance or Retirement Compensation Arrangement may be useful in reducing profits to the required level.

6. **The timing of the sale of your practice could save you tax, whether you're incorporated or not.** If you're not incorporated and have a calendar year-end, the best day to set as a closing date for the sale would be January 1st. Many of us have non-calendar year-ends, but everyone's personal year-end for tax purposes is December 31st. Let me explain further with an example.

CASE STUDY

Dr. S listed his practice in 2001 for $600,000. Subsequently, an interested purchaser made an acceptable offer for $592,500. Based on the allocation of various asset classes (goodwill, leaseholds, equipment, etc.) taxable income from the sale was estimated to be $320,000. The terms of sale did not require Dr. S to stay on in the practice as an associate for any length of time. In this case, Dr. S could leave whenever he wanted. Dr. S's fiscal year-end is the calendar year. During the year (2001), it was estimated that the practice would earn a net for Dr. S of $265,000. If the practice sale were to close in December of 2001, the total amount of taxable income the sale would generate would be taxed at 46.4% (the top rate at the time). That would mean tax on the sale without any planning, of $148,480. On the other hand, if the practice closing had been arranged for January 1, 2002, and it could also be arranged that Dr. S would have no other taxable income in 2002, then the tax payable would be about $12,000 less. That's not a bad savings for a one-day change!

7. **Timing can be a factor with an incorporated practice not selling shares but the assets of the practice.** If the corporation had a fiscal year end of July 31st (corporations can and do have non-calendar year ends), it would be possible to 'accrue' a bonus payable to you and/or your spouse in January of the following year. 'Accrued' means that provided it's paid out within six months the corporation can deduct it right away. This would reduce the corporation's tax for that year. The bonus wouldn't be taxable in your hands until the next taxation year at which point you ideally would have arranged your affairs so that it was subject to a low average tax rate. This strategy would appeal to a transitioning practitioner who found that the tax impact of the sale would mean their net corporate income would exceed the limit where the lower rate of corporate tax would apply (described above).

SECTION THREE: POST-TRANSITION TAX STRATEGIES

A great deal has been written about RRSP maturity options, CPP, OAS, and other forms of retirement income. In the interest of brevity, I won't comment on the mechanics of these sources of retirement funding, but instead focus on their implications for tax planning.

BARRY'S COACHING ADVICE

 Good post-transition tax strategies are the result of sound planning and organization in the pre-transition phase of your life. Whenever considering strategies suggested to you, ask about both the immediate impact and about how it will affect your tax position once you've retired. The best strategies have a long-term beneficial impact!

Old Age Security

One factor that can influence your post transition planning is Old Age Security (OAS). OAS is an indexed government program that provides income to all Canadians 65 or older. In 2004 the benefit, which is paid monthly, amounted to over $5,400 per year. That's in excess of $10,800 annually for two qualifying spouses. Over your retirement life, OAS benefits could add up to hundreds of thousands of dollars.

While OAS is potentially a great benefit, there is a proverbial fly in the ointment. In this case, it's a graduated claw-back of OAS benefits. As of this writing in 2003, OAS benefits start getting clawed back when the individual's taxable income exceeds $57,879. The benefit is completely clawed back when taxable income reaches $94,148 (again, for 2003). The OAS claw-back is based on your taxable income in the previous year. Should you be subject to the claw- back, it will be held back from ongoing payments as opposed to you having to write a cheque at the end of the year when you file your tax return.

Many retirement strategies are intended to help you save tax, and also leave you in a position to benefit from this government program. Therefore, it's important to plan your post- transition strategies so that you can take advantage of the OAS payments, if not forever, then at least for as long as possible. By using a combination of capital encroachment from sources of tax paid-capital and income from investments, RRSPs or pensions, corporate dividends and so on, it's possible for many retired practitioners to keep their taxable income below the claw-back level mentioned above. This means that not only can you enjoy the OAS income, but that your income taxes will be at a lower level.

Tax characteristics of various retirement capital pools

In your pre-transition planning, it's prudent to build capital, as mentioned earlier, with your post-transition needs in mind. These funds may be in RRSPs, IPPs, RCAs, corporations, insurance policies, and what can be thought of as open or non-registered investments. I think of each of these vehicles as pools of retirement capital. The tax characteristics of these "pools" of retirement capital are as follows:

a) **RRSPs must be converted to one of the approved alternatives in the year you turn age 69.** There are three broad categories of options to which you can convert your RRSP (assuming you aren't simply going to cash them in). The first is an Annuity and the second is a Registered Retirement Income Fund or RRIF as they're commonly referred to. The third is called a LIF, which stands for Life Income Fund. This is a maturity option for RRSPs that have been invested in insurance contracts such as segregated funds. Any income you receive from your RRSP directly or after you've converted it either to a RRIF, LIF, or Annuity is 100% taxable. If you have an IPP or if your spouse has a pension plan entitlement, the resulting income will be 100% taxable as well.

b) **Payments out of an RCA and pension are 100 per cent taxable.**

c) **Should you have funds built up in a corporation, when you take the money out it will be taxable as either dividends or salary or a mix of the two, depending on your circumstances.** If you have a professional corporation and/or a hygiene corporation, it may make sense to pay out some salary to both spouses so that you can continue to make RRSP contributions at least until the younger of you turns 69.

d) **Government benefits such as OAS and CPP are taxable as regular income to you.** The maximum Canada Pension Plan (CPP) benefit for 2003 was $9,615 annually, and like OAS the benefits are indexed. It's common for spouses not to qualify for the maximum

CPP benefit, and in cases such as this, it's possible to split your CPP benefit with your spouse. This can be a simple way to reduce your tax burden if your spouse is in a lower marginal income tax bracket than you.

e) **Capital gains and dividends are effectively taxed more favourably than interest income.**

f) **Using non-registered capital to support your retirement daily living needs doesn't create any tax in and of itself.** This makes non-registered capital an important planning tool.

g) **The equity you have in personal use assets such as your house or cottage can be strategically used in retirement to minimize tax.** This equity isn't taxable, so if there's no other non-registered capital to encroach on it may be possible to use some of these assets to supplement your cash flow. In this way, you won't have to take income from a taxable source that could put you into a much higher tax bracket or bring about a claw-back of your OAS benefits.

The assets could be used to access funds through an instrument such as a reverse mortgage or a home line of credit. I prefer these two alternatives to a traditional mortgage because the payments required by a normal amortization can impact your retirement cash flow. There's a way of using the equity you have in your personal use assets with borrowed money, where the interest is deductible. First, sell the investment assets (assuming you're not going to be triggering any big capital gain). Then, put the money in the bank or a money market fund to supplement your retirement cash flow, and borrow the funds to buy back the assets on the open market by using your personal-use asset as security.

Let me emphasize that borrowing should never be undertaken without a thorough analysis. Borrowing for investment purposes will increase your risk level. Before taking this step, review the strategy with your financial advisors. If you have an RCA, ask him or her about using the funds in the RCA Trust to put a mortgage on your home or cottage as a way of using these funds in a tax-efficient manner. From an estate planning perspective, if your health is good you may want to consider buying a term to 100 insurance policy (assuming you don't already have one) and assigning it to the bank. In that way, if something should happen to you, the loan would be paid off and the personal use asset would be free and clear for your survivor or heirs.

h)   **Borrowing against the CSV of your permanent life insurance contract can be a source of non-taxable cash.** Once again, the insurance portion of the contract would be assigned to the bank to pay off the loan when you pass on.

BARRY'S COACHING ADVICE

In late fall of each year, meet with your financial advisors to determine the following:

• what your income needs are likely to be over the coming calendar year

- what return expectations are likely to be

- if there have been any changes that will impact your retirement strategies

- the optimum use of your asset pools for the coming year in terms of withdrawals

Planning your retirement income on an annual basis is an important activity. It's your job to tell your advisor how much money you think you'll need in order to finance your expenditures. It's his or her job to figure out if you can afford to spend this sum, given your financial resources, and to work out the best withdrawal mix from the various pools of capital that are available to you, from a tax perspective.

Specific strategies for post-transition tax reduction

1.   **After age 60 you're entitled to a pension income tax credit.** If you don't have any pension income, take the $1,000 minimum

required from both your and your spouse's RRSPs and offset the tax liability with this pension income tax credit.

2.   **If you have non-registered investments that are generating so much income that you'll exceed the threshold for the OAS claw-back, ask your financial advisor to analyze the pros and cons of setting up a holding company into which you would transfer some or all of those income-producing assets.** The transfer could be accomplished on a tax-free basis using an election in the income tax act (ITA). The holding company is a separate taxpayer. It may help you to manage your income so that you avoid the claw-back.

3.   **If you're age 65 or older and your income is so high the OAS benefits are being clawed back, or if a significant portion of your assets have accrued gains on them, you may want to talk to your financial advisor about setting up an Alter Ego Trust.** This is a trust set up when you are alive to which you can transfer assets on a tax-deferred basis. Only you and your spouse should be entitled to receive any income or capital from the trust. This is a costly and complicated strategy and not for everyone. I recommend you go over it with your professional advisor.

4.   **If you have interest bearing investments outside of your registered plan, and investments such as stocks that earn capital gains and/or dividend income within your RRSP, you may want to consider exchanging them.** In this way, the interest income, rather than attracting tax as regular income, will benefit from the tax-free compounding available in the registered environment. Dividend income from Canadian corporations also qualifies for the dividend tax credit. When capital gains or dividends are earned in a registered environment, this tax advantage is lost. When possible, earn interest in the registered plans and dividends and capital gains outside such plans. Generally, you can make such changes either by selling your non- registered assets and using the cash to purchase the stocks or equity based mutual funds from the registered plan for Fair Market

Value, or you can do an exchange. If you elect to do an exchange, keep in mind that it must be at Fair Market Value. There's one important item to keep in mind in this situation. You can't deduct capital losses if the asset you're transferring to the registered plan is worth less than what you paid for it. Once again, check with your financial advisor to work out the mechanics.

5. **RRSPs must be converted to a RRIF, LIF, or Annuity by December 31st of the year that the annuitant turns 69.** If you've earned income in the year you turn age 69, you may want to consider making an over-contribution to your RRSP in late December. RRSP contributions are based on 18% of the prior year's earned income. As RRSP contributions can't be made after the year in which you turn 69, it's possible that you could lose the RRSP deduction capability for that year. Over-contributions to RRSPs are fined at the rate of 1% per month. The way the rules are currently written, by making an over-contribution in December, you would only have to pay the 1% penalty for one month. The following January you would be back on-side with the contribution rules.

6. **If you've earned income and are over the age of 69, it's no longer possible to make contributions to your own RRSP, but it is possible to make contributions to a spousal plan for your spouse if they're under the age of 70.**

7. **When you convert your RRSP to a RRIF, you don't have to start taking income right away.** In fact, you can delay it until the next year. Therefore, if you converted your RRSPs to a RRIF in September of 2004, you wouldn't have to take out any money until 2005. The longer you can leave that money in the registered plan, the greater the tax-free compounding benefit. If you don't need the money to live on, arrange for the minimal RRIF payment to be paid out until December of the year after you convert.

8. **The formula for calculating the minimum RRIF payment is age-**

dependant. The younger you are, the less money has to be paid out. You do have the option to base the RRIF payout formula either on your age or that of your spouse. If your spouse is younger than you are, basing the formula on his or her age will mean you have a lower minimum payout requirement. If you don't need the money to live on, this will reduce current taxes and leave more funds to compound tax-free for a longer period. Keep in mind that if you need more money in a given period, you can always increase the amount.

9. **A Prescribed Annuity can be an efficient way to earn tax-efficient income on interest bearing investments.** A Prescribed Annuity is not purchased with registered funds from an RRSP. In this case, you use non-registered funds. Prescribed Annuities offer a significant advantage. There are two components to the money paid out under a Prescribed Annuity. One is non-taxable cash flow. The other is the tax component. The nice feature of a Prescribed Annuity is that the taxable portion is often quite low. It can amount to a significant deferral when compared to holding a portion of your portfolio to supply your income needs in interest-bearing investments and paying the tax accordingly.

10. **If you change your Canadian residence, you may benefit from a lower or even a zero tax regulatory environment.** Canadians are taxed on residence, so if you're a Canadian resident, Canadian tax laws apply. Payments from your registered plans or an RCA may only be subject to a Canadian Withholding Tax, depending on the tax treaty with the country in which you reside. These withholding taxes may be substantially lower than the tax you would be faced with as a Canadian Resident. This is a very complex area and if you would like to explore it further, get a referral to a credible legal or accounting firm that specializes in this topic.

In summary, sound tax planning isn't always about one or two big actions that save buckets of tax. In fact, often tax planning involves a number of little 'bucket' strategies. Saving $5,000 here, $2,000 there, $7,000 elsewhere and so on adds up to real money. This is particularly true, thankfully, when you consider the cumulative impact over a number of years.

CHAPTER NINE

INVESTMENT STRATEGIES FOR TRANSITION

This chapter will help you:

- Understand the twelve principles or investment rules I've found to be most successful for dentists

- Understand what a formal investment strategy is and the benefits of using one

- Establish an investment strategy that complements your individual circumstances, constraints, and transition plans

INVESTMENT IS A CRITICAL PART OF YOUR TRANSITION PLANNING

An ideal final transition from your practice means you have an investment portfolio that will support your ongoing lifestyle needs. In other words, you have money working when you're not. Accumulating these resources is the first step, and we dealt with building the financial resources necessary for your individual needs in earlier chapters. Managing effectively what you have worked so hard to accumulate is equally important. Experience has taught me that certain approaches to investment management can be more successful than others—especially for members of the dental profession. What follows are comments, do's and don'ts, and recommended investment strategies customized for your profession.

CASE STUDY

To begin, let me relate a case from our files that can help illustrate the impact of investing on your transition plans. I met Dr. M in 2001,when he was 51-years old. He owned a productive and profitable practice and wanted to plan his transition for some time in his late fifties, or at age 60 at the latest. Dr. M had been married to Mrs. M for almost 25 years, and they had three children, one in university and two in high school.

While Dr. M had enjoyed a significant income all his practice life, a review of his financial affairs didn't reflect this. The RRSPs owned by he and his wife were not significant. There was comparatively little in the way of non-registered investments and they had a fair amount of debt. It was difficult to imagine where the money had gone. They had a nice house, yet it wasn't out of line for a family in their income bracket. Did they overspend on other lifestyle items? Give the money to charity? Gamble it away? No. It turns out the problem was investments.

As we talked about their finances, it became clear that over the years significant amounts of money had been lost on ill-considered investments. Dr. M had unsuccessfully 'played the market', and had also bought a number of tax shelters, some of which had not only lost significant amounts but had been reassessed by the tax department. He also had a fair amount of investment related debt. On the advice of his broker, he had borrowed money to invest in stocks during the heady days of the technology bubble. These funds had been invested in a limited number of speculative situations and had dropped precipitously once the bubble burst.

Dr. M's investment history indicated that he was a very aggressive investor. The problem was however, that neither Dr. M nor his wife fully understood the risks involved, and they weren't by nature 'risk takers'. In fact, a risk assessment indicated that they actually had a conservative to moderate investment profile.

Dr. M is an intelligent, accomplished person in his profession, but like so many others he had little training or experience to help him deal effectively in the investment arena. He didn't fully understand the risks he faced and how to manage them. He was also the victim of a system that in my view contains (and even promotes) a lot of myths and is rife with conflicts. A system that, outward appearances to the contrary, is not "investor friendly". Dr. M is not going to be able to reach his transition goals in the time frame he would have liked. But don't worry, he's just going to have to work a few more years. Had he invested more conservatively and not suffered such losses, our analysis indicated that he could have been in a position to work out of choice rather than necessity by his mid-fifties.

BARRY'S COACHING ADVICE

Learn and adhere to the Twelve Principles of Investing for Dentists outlined below.

TWELVE PRINCIPLES OF INVESTING FOR DENTISTS

After consulting with dentists for almost a quarter of a century on the management of their financial affairs, which by necessity includes their savings and investments, I've seen what works and what doesn't. Through this experience I've compiled a list of Twelve Principles I think you should consider for your investment program.

Principle One: The best investment most dentists will likely ever make is in their practice. This is the source of their fiscal strength. The most successful transition strategies build on this fact by emphasizing preservation of capital as a primary objective on their passive investments, and concentrating on generating wealth in the practice. In other words, when it takes so much effort and energy to make the money intended to pay for your financial security and future financial freedom, don't risk it.

Principle Two: Risk and reward in the investment world are intimately linked. The more return you want, the greater the risk you must undertake to earn it. In the investment world, risk is the premium you pay for greater return. When making investment decisions, don't concentrate on return or potential return alone. Always consider the downside. Ask the "What if" questions. Yes, all investments are subject to some form of risk or volatility. However, only undertake risk levels that are appropriate for your level of knowledge, risk tolerance, time horizons, investment objectives, and strategy.

Principle Three: It would be nice to think that your advisor (or anyone for that matter) knows what is likely to happen with interest rates, the economy, the stock market and so on. But the simple fact is, no one knows for sure. If anyone knew what was likely to happen with a high degree of reliability, they would be rich beyond compare. Yet pick up any business paper and you'll see convincing articles and commentary from credible sources that purport to do just that—predict the future. Each of these articles supports their thesis with logic that sounds well thought out and researched. Yet such articles commonly express opinions that are completely opposite to opinions in other, equally scholarly writings. It can be confusing to say the least.

It most often takes a great deal of specialized training, experience, and education to be able to even hope to evaluate the wisdom of one investment opinion over another. Few practitioners really have the time for this. Instead, when you understand that no one can predict what's going to happen in the investment arena with any consistency, you'll be armed with insight that's far more potent. This knowledge will allow you to take a long-term view of your investments, without being stressed by the 'opinion de jour'.

Market timing is one of the major reasons that many investors use the articles mentioned in the previous paragraph. However, let me tell you that study after study has shown that neither pundits nor investors, even sophisticated ones, can effectively time the market consistently: i.e. pick the right time to go into the market and the right time to get out. Markets tend to move in spurts. Large changes can take place virtually in a single day. These moves happen so fast it's impossible to consistently predict them in time. For example, if you had invested $1,000 in the S&P 500 (an American stock index) in 1951 and been able to predict when to get into the market and when to get out and been right 100% of the time, your $1,000 would have grown to $392,680,727 by the year 2000. That is a handsome sum by anyone's criteria. If you were right only 75% of the time, that $1,000 would have grown to $3,335,443. This is still a lot of money, but what a difference that 25% makes!

Interestingly, the next best alternative would have been to take a long-term view and not try to time the markets. In this case, your $1,000 would have grown to $56,851 in the time period. If you had been right only 50% of the time, your $1,000 would be worth less than half of what it would have been worth by staying invested all the time. If you were right only 25% of the time, you would have lost money! The economic, political and investment worlds are just too complex to expect that you'll be able to make accurate market timing decisions with the consistency required for success.

Let's look at another statistic. From January of 1990 to December of 2001, the Dow average yearly return was 10.25%. If you guessed wrong and were out of this market during the best 40 days (there were over 4,000 days during this period), your return would have been a negative .49%. Similar studies have been done on the Toronto Stock Exchange (TSX) and the results have been the same. The top money managers in the world, trained and experienced professionals who have access to in-depth research material, cannot consistently time markets. Even if it was possible for you to consider market timing as part of your investment strategy, it would require a great deal of research to sort through the plethora of economic data that you would need to assess. In my experience, most independent professionals are simply too busy to do this considering the demands of a busy practice, family time and trying to have a personal life.

For the transitioning dentist, the most successful approach is to have an investment strategy in place that takes a long-term view, and no matter what happens—follow the plan. This may be challenging because things such as fear and greed influence our human emotions – yet history has shown that this is your best option. When dealing with the financial members of your transition advisory team, insist on diversified strategies that aren't dependent on short-term trends or events for success.

Principle Four: The investment field is full of conflicts and it's important that you understand them. A few years ago, the U.S. Securities and Exchange Commission formed a committee on the future of the investment industry. It was called the Tulley Commission after Dan Tulley, chairman of Merrill Lynch at the time. This committee felt that the prevailing commission-based compensation system within the industry didn't provide value to investors. They went on to say that if they could redesign the business, it would be on a fee - based consultative process as opposed to the commission driven transaction based model. This is not to say that advisors who are compensated on a commission basis don't act ethically. Quite the contrary. There are many commission-based advisors who are professional and highly ethical. I have great empathy for anyone in the investment field who has to make their living on straight commission. There can be enormous pressures to trade actively. If they don't, how do they finance their lifestyle, pay for their children's education, the mortgage and so on? Unfortunately, this can lead to the problem of not knowing whether a commission-compensated advisor is making recommendations motivated by what's in your best interest, or by big commissions.

While I believe that working with a fee-for-service advisor is generally the best choice, it's important to keep in mind that conflicts exist in every business and profession. That applies to fee-based investment arrangements as well. Just because you are paying a fee, be it an hourly rate, a flat fee, or a percentage of assets, it is in your best interest to make sure you understand them. For example, where possible work with a fee-for-service advisor who has access to all forms of investments, not just proprietary products.

Principle Five: Whether you are dealing with a fee-for-service or commission-driven advisor, it's important to make sure they're qualified. Someone wanting to become a broker in Canada today needs only to pass the Canadian Securities Course (CSC), taken by correspondence, and fulfill some other regulatory requirements such as passing the Conduct and Practices exam and registering with the appropriate securities and industry regulators. The CSC, offered by the Canadian Securities Institute is a good basic course.

However, you should be dealing with someone who has more qualifications than just the basics. Having an MBA, an accounting designation, or even a PhD doesn't necessarily mean the person has advanced training in the investment world. Look for a combination of related designations. The CFP (Certified Financial Planner) is a desirable designation and provides training for working with a client's overall financial circumstances. Your investment portfolio isn't a stand alone aspect of your finances, in the same way that your leg isn't separate from the rest of your body. Integration is very important. Someone with a CFP must also adhere to a strict code of ethics and standards. As well, CFPs are required to obtain a minimum of 30 hours of education credits per year to keep their knowledge-base current.

In addition to the CSC and CFP, an advisor needs more advanced training on investment. A CIM (Certified Investment Manager) or CFA (Certified Financial Analyst) designation is a good indication that your advisor has furthered his or her education in investment management and strategies. There are many other designations that an advisor can earn, and the effort they have put into acquiring advanced, specialized qualifications is a good indication of their abilities. I should point out there's a lot of controversy within the financial community on qualifications. Some argue that there are designations and qualifications that are as good as the CFP, and they may well be right, but I have very little personal knowledge of these other courses.

The point I am making here is that it's the combination of the CSC, CFP, and CIM or CFA – as opposed to any one designation – that's a good indicator of who is and who isn't qualified to be the investment member of your transition advisory team. I must admit that I possess some of these designations and have something of a conflict of interest or bias. The bias is intentional. I have spent a lot of time researching what courses of study provide the best tools for working with clients on their financial affairs.

Principle Six: Choosing to work with an advisor that has a desirable combination of qualifications is only part of the job. I believe that the best way to work with any advisor is to delegate the investment management of your portfolio, as opposed to abdicating authority for it. After all, this is your money and your future. You have a right to ask a lot of questions. It's important you understand and agree with the strategy, and feel that it fits well with your overall transition planning. If you don't understand it, don't invest in it. If your advisor can't explain it to your satisfaction, well…

Principle Seven: Manage on a portfolio basis as opposed to an asset-by-asset basis. This relates back to my earlier comment that no one knows what's going to happen in the future. Diversification is an excellent way of dealing with this fact. If done properly, a portfolio should include a mix of assets that react differently to economic, political and market conditions. At any one time some assets may be up, others may be down. By managing on a portfolio basis, you place the emphasis on obtaining the overall yield or return you need at the risk level that's appropriate to your circumstances. There are a couple of books you may want to review that can give you some more insight on this topic. They are *Risk is Still a Four Letter Word* by George Hartman and *Secrets of Successful Investing* by Gordon Pape and Eric Kirzner.

Principle Eight: Over the last few years, short-term volatility has increased dramatically. If you can't invest for the long term, only put your money into something safe and sure. Consider for example, T-bills, GICs, or government bonds with a weighted maturity under five years. Otherwise, you may find that you need to cash in investments that are volatile in nature at the wrong time, when things are down. It's a proven fact that time horizon plays a critical role in investment success.

Principle Nine: Don't look at your portfolio in isolation. In the investment world, everything is relative. In demonstrating this point to clients, I often ask the question, "In a given year is an 8% return good or bad?" The answer depends on comparisons. If an investment with a similar level of risk earned 6% during the same period, it's a great return. On the other hand if another comparable investment earned 10%, then the 8% result isn't that good. A practical resource for making such comparisons are the various indexes that are published in any reputable business publication and on certain Internet websites.

Principle Ten: Don't take risks with the fixed income (bonds, guaranteed investment certificates, mortgage backed securities and so on) component of your portfolio. I mentioned the importance of diversification earlier. Each investment strategy should contain some fixed income, which is the component of your portfolio that represents a stabilizing force for your investment strategy. Most people are unaware that fixed income is subject to a number of different types of risk.

One key type is interest rate risk. If you had a 30-year Government of Canada bond in your portfolio, paying say 6% and interest rates increased so that bonds of similar credit risk and term were earning 8%, what do you think would happen to the resale value of your bond? It would drop dramatically in value. Who's going to pay you one hundred cents on the dollar for your bond to get a 6% rate of return, when they can buy someone else's for the same price and get 8%?

The only way you could sell that bond is if the price was adjusted downward so that the 6% on the face of the bond equalled 8% on the actual price the purchaser paid.

BARRY'S COACHING ADVICE

 Invest in high quality credit risks only and keep your average maturity to five years (shorter maturities are less sensitive to interest rate volatility).

Principle Eleven: If you're considering mutual funds or some other form of managed money concept such as working with an investment counselor, exclude compound performance from your selection criteria. It can be very misleading. Let's say you were evaluating a mutual fund that had been in existence for three years. The first year it made 50%. The second year it lost 5% and the third year it lost 15%. Obviously, this is not a good trend. Yet its compound rate of return would still be 10% per year.

Year-by-year performance statistics are readily available, and they can give you a clear picture of the track record of the particular investment vehicle you're considering. They also make comparisons with similar managers and appropriate indexes much easier. However, don't buy last year's winner. If a mutual fund or a particular sector of the market did really well last year, don't kick yourself for not buying in earlier and then move quickly to remedy the situation.

If a stock or mutual fund drastically exceeded general market performance in a given year, statistics show that buying it now is not a good decision. Chances are you'll be either too late and performance from here on in will be lack-luster, or you could even incur a loss. The old expression "what goes up must come down" very often applies to last year's top performers in the investment world!

In addition, don't invest in a mutual fund that has a track record that is less than three years old. To make an informed decision you need to compare the performance of the fund to similar funds and to appropriate indexes. A lot has been written about Management Expense Ratios. They can reduce your effective returns if the performance isn't there to justify the cost, or if you're not getting value for your money. When you buy a mutual fund, you're effectively hiring a supposedly experienced investment manager. Without access to at least three years of performance criteria on that particular fund, how are you to make an assessment?

The sales pitch on new mutual funds often relates to the great track record of a manager who worked on another fund or fund family. You can't rely on this. The previous company could have had a different decision-making process, more or less supervision, better or worse research capabilities, and a variety of other factors that could influence performance.

Principle Twelve: My final guideline would be to understand the many risks you face as an investor. Some of them aren't always that obvious …

Let's look at the types of risks you face as an investor

Systematic Risk, sometimes called market risk, can affect all portfolios regardless of quality. Many people think of market risk as exclusively applying to the stock market. But it's important to recognize that this also applies to the fixed income market. Systematic risk addresses movements in broad markets. You could own the best in blue chip stocks, but if the market declines as a whole, then the value of all stocks will decline. Similarly, if the broad market increases, those blue chip stocks would likely increase in value right along with the rest. The point here is that these movements have nothing to do with the specific investment. The volatility actually relates to factors that affect various markets as a whole, such as good or bad economic news. Unfortunately, owning blue chip stocks won't protect your portfolio from unwanted volatility.

Systematic Risk is one of the reasons you need to diversify your portfolio. Different types of assets such as stocks, cash or near cash (money markets), fixed income, etc., don't necessarily react in the same way to outside stimuli. When the stock market declines it's not uncommon to see an improvement in fixed income assets. This is because general markets work somewhat on a supply and demand basis. When stock markets start to decline, investors fear they will lose money and demand is reduced. In times of uncertainty, investors often look for security. In doing this, much of the money from the sale of stocks is put into fixed income alternatives. Therefore, demand increases. They don't perfectly offset each other, but having your portfolio diversified between types of assets can help ease volatility.

Unsystematic Risk, or company specific risk, represents another reason that you should manage your investments on a portfolio basis and diversify your portfolio. Think about the once great companies that have fallen on hard times. We've all heard the old adage "Don't put all your eggs in one basket". The concept definitely applies here. While opinions differ, many investment professionals believe you need somewhere between 20 and 30, or even more companies in a stock portfolio to properly address systematic risk.

To add additional protection against volatility, these companies should be diversified by industry (it's possible for an industry to go into a slump) and geographic location. Choosing the appropriate companies for such a portfolio demands a lot of expertise and hard work. Think about the information you would want to see to buy another ongoing practice for cash. You would need details on financial performance, costs, service mix, employees and on and on and on. When you're adding a company to your portfolio, you're fundamentally buying a business. To make sure you're making the right decision, you should do a thorough analysis of the company in question. You'll also have to monitor their suitability on an ongoing basis. The fact that it takes so much effort is one of the reasons why mutual funds and managed investment alternatives are popular.

Inflation risk, or risk to your spending power, must also be addressed. This is particularly true when you're constructing a portfolio while contemplating your transition. You may well be living off that portfolio longer than you had actually worked!

If today you spend $75,000 per year after-tax to maintain your lifestyle, then ten years from now, at 3 per cent inflation, you'll need $100,793 to buy the same goods and services. In 20 years you'll need $135,458. The best way to deal with inflation is to own assets within your portfolio that will grow on an-after tax basis at a rate that is higher than inflation. This is one of the main reasons you need an investment strategy. If it wasn't for the long-term negative effects of inflation you could leave all your money in assets that are very safe and sure such as treasury bills. When tax and inflation are considered, treasury bills can often experience negative real growth – in other words, lose purchasing power.

Exchange rate risk is another possible area of volatility. During the summer of 2003, the US greenback substantially declined in value relative to the Canadian dollar. If, at that time, you had all or substantially all of your transition assets denominated in US dollars, their current value would have declined dramatically. Once again, being diversified is the answer.

Credit risk is similar to unsystematic risk in that it's company specific. In this case, it applies to fixed income. Governments and corporations, including financial institutions such as banks, issue debt of various kinds. Credit risk for governments in Canada and the United States are generally thought to be very low.

In Canada, when dealing with the credit risk on bank deposits and securities like GICs, you don't need to be concerned about any credit risk up to $60,000 because of the guarantee of the Canadian Depository Insurance Corporation. Other debt, such as corporate debt, may not be as secure. Fortunately, there are ratings available on most debt from companies like the Dominion Bond Rating Service and Moodys, that will give you guidance for your decisions.

Political risk can also affect your portfolio. I'm not just talking about things like the September 11th attack in the United States. Regulatory changes can also have a serious effect on some industries. Political interference is another concern. An example is the National Energy Program, which ultimately resulted in investors in the Oil and Gas sector experiencing significant declines in share values.

Additional risks faced by dentists

Management time.

I've seen a number of clients, with very successful practices, who have decided they would invest in something that required active management. Frequently, it's rental real estate. One client bought into a small company started by a long-time friend and patient. The original deal was that there would be no management time required by my client (incidentally, he became my client well after acquiring his interest in this company). Unfortunately, things did not go very well. Not only did the friendship run into problems, but also my client had to step in and start taking an active role in the business. He had a large part of his net worth tied up in this company so if he didn't devote his time there was a risk that his investment would be lost. It was clear when reviewing his practice financial statements from a number of years, the exact year he had to start devoting time to this company.

In the end, the investment didn't make money and the hidden cost was the loss of income from the practice. Income declined because the practitioner's focus was elsewhere. Direct ownership of real estate can also have a material drain on your available time. Negotiating rents, collecting rents, maintenance, repairs, dealing with mortgages and everything else involved can take a large part of your emotional energy. Energy that would probably be more profitably devoted to your practice.

The possibility of making a costly error.

It would be foolish of me to treat myself for a serious illness or look after my own dental health. I don't have the training or the experience to be a physician or dentist. In the same way, it takes many years of education, experience and training to become an investment professional.

As an exception to the rule, there are people who do a good job managing their own investments. In my experience, these success stories fall into two categories. In the first category, the person is very interested in the investment process, works hard at it, has educated themselves, and has gained valuable experience. In the other case, the individual recognizes their limitations and works with a simple investment strategy, where management fits into his or her schedule.

In the investment world there's something called the Efficient Market Theory. This theory contends that all information generally available to the investing public has been factored into the price of a particular asset like a stock or mutual fund. There is naturally some controversy surrounding the validity of the Efficient Market Theory, but a number of studies seem to support it. Even those who don't agree with it acknowledge that in general, it takes a lot of work and investment know-how to identify undervalued opportunities in advance of the market. For busy practitioners who aren't investment professionals, I believe it's reasonable to accept the Efficient Market Theory concept and invest for the long term.

The risk of not having your money when you need it.

Many dentists have aggressive investments in their portfolios. As mentioned earlier in this chapter, risk and reward are intimately linked. The greater the reward you try to achieve, the greater the risk you must undertake to obtain that reward. That's the trade off. Greater reward goes to those who are willing to assume greater risk. It's something of a conundrum. You want to invest aggressively to grow your assets as much as possible. Yet because of the increased risk, you endanger your financial security. If you end up losing money, it's extremely hard to make it back.

> *The place to create wealth is in your practice, and the purpose of wealth management is to first hang onto the wealth you create and to second, obtain a reasonable rate of real growth (after tax and inflation).*

The need for a formal investment strategy

One of the key reasons you need to have a formal investment strategy is to help you manage the many risks you face. A cornerstone of Modern Portfolio Theory is diversification. Harry Markowitz, a Nobel Prize winning mathematician, proved it was possible to reduce risks and in some cases simultaneously improve returns through diversification. Another mathematician, Gary Brinson, named one of the four most influential investors in the world in 1993, found that the most important contributor to investment success wasn't asset selection (what stocks to pick, etc.) or market timing, but rather the decision to diversify. He found that the decision to diversify contributed an overwhelming 90% to investment success. Later studies have supported these conclusions and in some cases attributed an even greater amount of weight to the asset allocation decision. By the way, asset allocation is the buzzword within the investment community applied to the concept of planned diversification in the construction of investment strategies.

Another benefit of using a formal investment strategy is that it helps to take the emotion out of investing. Emotions such as fear of loss or desire for additional profits can have a material impact on such decisions as, "When should I buy? Is a 5% return satisfactory? Should I hold on until the return goes up to 10% or 15% or more? When is the right time to sell an investment that has experienced a loss?" These are difficult decisions. Ideally, investment should be a methodical, disciplined process, which demands a formal strategy approach.

Finally, a formal investment strategy helps you monitor results and make appropriate and timely adjustments to your portfolio. When you prepare your investment strategy, expectations are established, such as the expected range of return and volatility level. Once you have reasonable expectations, the actual performance of the strategy can be compared with those expectations. It also becomes possible to gauge the strategy's performance by comparing it to appropriate benchmarks or indexes. Being able to monitor results and make appropriate comparisons is really the essence of control.

Establishing your investment strategy

First let me summarize the principles or rules of investing that in my experience work best for dental practitioners, as defined earlier:

1) Recognize that Wealth Creation is a practice activity, while Wealth Management is what your investment strategy should do.

2) Keep in mind that risk and reward are linked. The higher the reward, the higher the risk.

3) Remember that no one knows what's going to happen in the

future. You'll be faced with many risks as an investor. Diversification is the key, so that no matter what happens there is a higher expectation that you'll have your money when you need it.

4) Studies show that market timing does not work consistently.

5) The investment world is full of conflicts. Make sure you understand them before making your investment decisions.

6) If an investment professional is a member of your advisory team, make sure he or she is properly qualified and if possible, deal with someone that works on a fee-for-service basis.

7) If a qualified investment professional is a member of your transition advisory team, delegate but don't abdicate.

8) Manage your assets on a portfolio basis as opposed to asset by asset. Nothing will ever be up or down all the time. The trick is to build your portfolio with assets that complement or offset each other.

9) Invest for the long term.

10) Don't look at individual investments or your portfolio in isolation. Compare performance to appropriate benchmarks.

11) Don't take risks with the Fixed Income portion of your portfolio. Invest in high quality credit risks, vary your maturities so that you are reinvesting approximately 20% of your fixed income portfolio every year, and keep the weighted average maturities of your fixed income assets to five years or under.

12) Don't use compound rates of return as performance criteria in your specific asset selection process. Year-by-year performance is much more useful. Also, look for consistent performance instead of chasing last year's big winners.

Asset allocation and your investment strategy

There's an order to the way one should formulate an investment strategy. Many books written about investment start with establishing specific goals, then continue with a discussion on determining risk tolerance levels, followed by a discussion on the importance of time horizons. I'm going to diverge from this standard because this book is on transition planning for the dental profession, and therefore not general in nature. Also, Chapter One is devoted to goal setting. So let's start by assuming that your goals are already in place and your risk tolerance level is conservative. The first step is to decide how your assets will be diversified – the Asset Allocation Plan – for your portfolio. Listed below are the three broad asset classes from which to choose, along with what I would consider to be their risk profile.

1. Cash (bank deposits, Tbills) or near cash (secure money markets, Government of Canada bonds with a maturity under one year). LOW RISK.

2. Fixed Income investments, such as GICs or bonds, with quality credit risks and an average maturity of five years or under. LOW TO MODERATE RISK.

3. Diversified portfolio of equities. MODERATE TO HIGH RISK ON HOLDING PERIODS (TIME HORIZONS) OF LESS THAN FIVE TO TEN YEARS.

Having dealt with all of the above, you now have two choices. You can establish your plan yourself, or you can make a qualified investment professional a member of your transition advisory team. My advice, frankly, would be to hire a professional to help with the design of the strategy, even if you want to manage it yourself. For those who are establishing their own investment strategy, be sure to pick up a good book on the topic. I mentioned a couple earlier.

If you're working with an advisor, make sure they put forth enough time and effort to gain a complete understanding of your overall financial circumstances, your goals, risk tolerance levels, time horizons, and other constraints if any. Your investment professional should be able to demonstrate how the recommended asset allocation model has performed historically over the last one, three, five, ten, and fifteen -year period. Databases are readily available to investment professionals for this purpose. Also, ask that the performance of the proposed asset allocation model be compared in a graph format, for the periods mentioned above, against appropriate indexes so that you can see how it performed on a comparative basis.

After your advisor has produced an asset allocation model that is to your satisfaction, it's necessary to pick the specific assets that will populate the various categories in your model. The selection criteria should be governed by the fact that you'll be monitoring the portfolio's performance relative to the indexes. Your expectation is that your portfolio will do as well as or better than the portfolio of indexes. If the assets in the various categories do not perform as well as the index, then this is an indication that a change is necessary. In many cases it may just be prudent to buy the indexes themselves. This can be done with mutual funds that replicate the indexes or with instruments such as iUnits (an iUnit is the Canadian member of the global family of exchange-traded funds from Barclays Global Investors).

Monitoring your investment strategy and ongoing rebalancing

Your asset allocation will have to be rebalanced regularly, and I recommend quarterly. This is important because change is inevitable. Let's say that in one month your Canadian Equity component had gone up dramatically. It's supposed to represent 10% of your portfolio under your asset allocation plan. Now, because of this increase it represents 20%. This is what's called "portfolio drift". If you don't sell off 10% of those equities and redistribute the monies into the other categories so the portfolio is brought back into line with the allocation plan, you will lose control of your strategy and can no longer expect that it will perform in the manner for which it was designed.

There's another advantage in rebalancing. Most investors sell low and buy high. In effect, this system of management attempts to reverse that process. When one area of the portfolio is up, it must be sold and the funds invested in an area that's down. This system helps to provide you with the discipline necessary to have you selling high and buying low.

In addition to rebalancing on a quarterly basis, I recommend you have your investment professional prepare a comparison showing how the various indexes representing your asset allocation model performed in the same period. Did you do better, worse, or the same? If you did better or the same, then it's reasonable to assume the strategy is working as anticipated during the period under review. If it didn't perform as well, you should be able to determine why. Then you'll need to make a decision about whether it's necessary to change some of the specific holdings that make up your asset category, in order to achieve the performance you expect and want.

CHAPTER TEN

RISK MANAGEMENT

This chapter will help you:

- Develop a philosophy to guide your insurance strategies

- Understand the various types of insurance and assess your need for coverage

- See the benefits of practice contingency planning, including office overhead insurance

- Understand other important information related to this topic

G iven time and proper planning, most dentists have the *potential* to build a relative level of financial security and success. I'm emphasizing the word *potential* because, as the saying goes, "Life is what happens while you're making other plans". Unfortunately this means that in any population group, such as dentists, statistics show that a certain percentage of people will experience some form of calamity for which the financial consequences are significant. Such calamities happen at random, and they can affect anyone. Now, chances are you'll be one of the lucky ones, but there's no way to be absolutely sure. Some catastrophe could happen to you or a member of your family. Therefore, it's only prudent that your transition strategies include planning for contingencies.

Risk management is a very important topic, yet there's a lot of confusion surrounding how to go about formulating appropriate, coordinated strategies. This is particularly true of risk management strategies that involve insurance. So it's my hope that this chapter will help to clarify this important topic.

Why it's important to establish your own philosophy about insurance

Insurance can be both complex and expensive. But worse than that, insurance policies can be pretty dull to read. These complicated, difficult to understand contracts create a barrier that can reduce the ability of dentists to be informed consumers of insurance products. Also, there are so many insurance products available that it can feel as if there are a limitless number of variations. Who has the time or legal training to read all these contracts and fully understand the benefits of one variation over another?

Insurance can also be a major expense for a dental family – particularly as most premiums have to be paid from after-tax dollars. And if you never have to make a claim, paying them can feel like a waste of money. So, where is the satisfaction from paying that expensive premium? You don't get much in the way of "pizzazz" for your insurance dollar. It's not like you can reach out and touch it, put it in your living room and admire it, or take it for a spin on a pleasant summer day. In addition, your resources are finite, which means if you spend money on insurance coverage that you don't really need, those funds won't be available for other important things in your life.

There are also many potential conflicts in the way insurance is sold in Canada today. Don't misunderstand. There are many capable and ethical insurance agents in the marketplace, and I have respect for what they do. It's only that these potential conflicts are one more reason why it's important that you establish your own insurance philosophy. It's the only way you can hope to control the process and be sure that you're getting value for the money you put towards premiums.

How to establish your insurance philosophy

Start with the premise that the purpose of insurance is first and foremost to protect you against being that one in the population group who is impacted by life's random events. Next, adopt the KIS principle – "Keep it Simple". Perhaps I can explain more effectively what I mean by relating this philosophy to buying a car. You can purchase a luxury vehicle with all the bells and whistles, or if you simply want basic transportation, you can buy a less expensive automobile that still does the job of getting you from A to B.

When you apply this example to insurance, paying that extra money for the luxury model won't give you the pleasure you would get from a fully-loaded, luxury automobile. So philosophically it makes sense to concentrate on acquiring and maintaining coverage that takes you from A to B. This means insuring risks with the simplest alternatives possible. I'm talking about risks you can't afford to underwrite yourself. Now having said all that, I do believe that insurance is a necessity, and I don't mean to imply that you should buy only the cheapest. Assessing your need is an individual process. Once you've decided on your insurance philosophy, it's important to communicate it to your agents when considering a proposal or obtaining quotes. Get competing quotations (not from the same agent, even if he or she states that they can survey all the insurance companies for the best product). Finally, insist that as part of the quotation the agent shows you how their proposal complies with your philosophical approach to insurance.

CASE STUDY

 One of my clients has seen his practice income grow dramatically over the last couple of years. Given this higher income, his insurance agent felt he should increase his disability insurance and provided him with a proposal. If the client went ahead, it would mean a significant increase in the annual premium.

By way of background, this client is in good financial shape. He and his wife have always had a lifestyle that costs significantly less than their income. As a result, they have no debt and have accumulated a sizable investment portfolio. My client's definition of the risk of disability was not being able to provide for his current lifestyle needs and future financial security.

After reviewing the proposal with my client and relating it to his unique financial picture, I recommended he decline the offer of additional coverage. He was in complete agreement that he didn't need to spend money insuring his income. The fact was that he already had sufficient disability coverage to provide for his wants and his current lifestyle needs. Further analysis indicated, with a high level of confidence, that his portfolio was sufficient to provide for his retirement needs if it was left to grow until he was 65. Age 65 is when his disability benefit would run out in the case of a claim. His present coverage would be adequate to provide for his lifestyle before retirement, and he already had a nest egg for the future. It was even decided that we would change the elimination period on his policy from 60 days to a much longer period. This reduced his current premium by a significant amount. He had the cash reserves to handle a short-term disability, so in effect he was paying for coverage he didn't need.

Life Insurance

Of the various types of insurance you may require, the most fundamental is life insurance. Ben Feldman, a famous insurance man with *New York Life* once said, "The basic purpose of life insurance is to create cash...nothing more...and nothing less". Should the person insured under the contract die, the insurance company pays out cash either to the named beneficiaries or to the estate. To determine how much insurance you would need, keep in mind that life insurance for dental practitioners is typically required for the following risks:

1. Ongoing lifestyle needs for your spouse and family
2. Funding your children's education
3. Retiring outstanding debt
4. Providing funding to partners, cost sharing associates, or members of your self-protection group to purchase your practice interests
5. Paying for taxes as a result of the insured's demise (capital gains, recapture)
6. Covering estate legal and administrative needs
7. Leaving a specified sum for your heirs

8. Leaving money to a charity or religious group

So, how much coverage do you need?

Some people feel that you can never have too much life insurance. Interestingly, most of the people who feel this way are insurance agents. Of course, you can't blame them for being enthusiastic about what they sell. However, you'll have to decide what's right for your own circumstances.

My recommendation is, as mentioned above, that you buy enough life insurance to cover the risks that you don't have the ability to underwrite yourself. This means you have to work out or effectively quantify those risks with a financial member of your transition advisory team (not someone who's selling you insurance) prior to meeting with your insurance agent.

Three steps for working out your need for life insurance

Step One: Estimate your needs today.

Specifically, make estimates on:
- Final expenses such as funeral and burial costs
- Paying off all debt, including practice loans and leases
- Emergency cash needs of your family until insurance is paid out and the estate settled
- Total education costs for your children
- Living costs of your spouse and family until your spouse's retirement and other family members are independent
- How much capital your spouse will need to finance his or her retirement
- The amount you would like to leave to charity, religious affiliations, or other estate wishes, such as leaving a specific amount to your heirs, providing money to keep the cottage in the family, and so on.

Step Two: Estimate what you already have to meet those needs.

Specifically, make estimates on:
- Investment assets such as RRSPs and savings
- Income your surviving spouse might expect to earn
- Insurance already in place

Note: I don't include the value of a practice in the assets unless there's a good practice contingency plan in place such as a solid buy-sell arrangement. It's difficult to estimate the price that your heirs could reasonably expect if the practice must be sold under distressed circumstances.

Step Three: Deduct the total arrived at from your calculations in Step Two from the needs you worked out in Step One.

A deficit should equal the amount of insurance coverage you need. If there's a surplus, you'll have to decide whether or not you're getting value for such coverage. I find that many of my clients, as they approach transition, become self-insured.

This analysis should be performed for both husband and wife, as well as for an event of joint disaster, to make sure your needs and wishes are addressed for any eventuality.

Types of Life Insurance

Generally life insurance falls into two broad categories, Term Insurance and Permanent Insurance. The two are quite different. It may help to think of the differences in the following way. With Term Insurance you're basically renting the coverage you need, and with Permanent Life Insurance, you're buying it.

Term Insurance

Term Insurance provides coverage for a specific period of time such as 5, 10, or 20 years or to age 100. At the end of that period of time, the policy will expire without any cash value unless you renew it. Generally this form of life insurance is less expensive when you're younger and increases in cost as you age. I find it particularly well suited for many of my clients because they typically need the largest amount of coverage at the time when the most demands are being made on their cash flow.

In examining a client's insurance needs, I often find they look like a bell curve on a chart. For example, when their family is young, debts tend to be heavy because they're paying off their home and establishing their practice, etc. As they age, debts decline, the amount of time they have to provide for the lifestyle needs of their surviving spouse and children is reduced, and their assets build. Eventually it's possible that their assets will grow to the point that they become self-insured from a risk of premature death.

As an aside, I often wonder why the insurance industry doesn't refer to Term to 100 as Permanent Insurance. It certainly seems like permanent coverage. The only difference is that it doesn't build up cash surrender value, but it also costs a whole lot less.

BARRY'S COACHING ADVICE

When buying Term Insurance, two options (bells and whistles) I'd recommend are:

1) It should be Guaranteed Renewable without evidence of insurability, to eliminate the concern over renewing coverage if there's been a change in your health.

2) It should be Guaranteed Convertible in case a reason develops in the future why you must have permanent coverage.

Permanent Insurance

Permanent Insurance is intended to provide coverage for your entire life, and it's often referred to as Whole Life or Universal Life. There are two components to this form of life insurance. One is the insurance coverage and the other is a savings component.

Permanent Insurance generally involves a level premium either for your whole life or for a specific period of time, such as 20 years. Typically these costs are significantly higher than comparable term coverage, when you're young. At some point as you get older, there's a crossover where the annual premium cost for term coverage becomes greater than the level premium of the permanent policy alternative. When making a choice between permanent coverage and term coverage, I've often heard the argument made by insurance agents that the level premium permanent coverage is actually cheaper because of the high cost of maintaining a term policy in later life.

If you want to compare the cost of term versus level premium permanent coverage, have your financial advisor (not the one selling the insurance contract) do a "present value" analysis of the two premium payment streams. This is a mainstream form of financial analysis that compares different future inflows and outflows (the future cash surrender value). The assumption is that a dollar today is worth much more than a dollar in the future. For example at 3% inflation, a dollar payable 20 years from now is really worth about 55 cents in present value terms.

Permanent Insurance may be a better consideration than term coverage because…

You can use it to pay the income tax arising on death

On your death there's a deemed disposition of all your assets. Depending on the makeup of your net worth, that would typically mean tax on any capital gains existing at the time of your passing, and tax from having all of your RRSPs or RRIFs deemed as income at that point. In Canada there are regulatory provisions that allow, on the death of one spouse, for non-registered assets to be transferred to the surviving spouse at the adjusted cost base of the deceased. Likewise, there are spousal rollover provisions for your RRSP (the spouse should be the named beneficiary for your RRSPs, and it's also a good idea to include a clause to that effect in your will).

These rollover provisions allow the surviving spouse to transfer any RRSP or RRIF assets directly into their own plans without paying any immediate tax. The result is that tax on capital gains or on RRSP assets can be effectively deferred until the passing of the surviving spouse. That leaves three potential scenarios where you might want to consider permanent life insurance to pay tax on death:

1) If you're single and want to preserve the pre-tax value of your estate.

2) If you're married and want to preserve the pre-tax value of your estate, consider the permanent policy on a "joint last to die" basis, where both spouses are covered and the insurance benefits aren't paid until the death of the surviving spouse.

3) You have an asset such as a family cottage that you want to make sure remains in your family, and a significant capital gain has built up. Once again, because of the spousal rollover provisions you may want to consider such coverage on a "joint last to die" basis.

Savings in a Permanent Insurance policy can grow tax-free

One of the selling points often promoted as a reason to buy Permanent Insurance is the potential for tax-free growth of the cash surrender value. Provided the amount of insurance relative to the investment component of the policy is in compliance with a government formula, the investment component grows tax-free. Both insurance companies and agents enthusiastically promote this feature. In a profession like dentistry where you typically carry more than your proportional share of the Canadian tax burden, such a feature may be music to your ears. However, you should take a close look before you sign.

After policy taxes, administration charges, selling costs, high management fees for some of their investment alternatives and the cost of the insurance, the tax-free benefit may not be so great. This is particularly true when the investment growth is compared to other alternatives, even when you factor in the tax. Many permanent life insurance contracts are sold with the idea that the policyholder will use the built up cash surrender value in retirement as security for a loan to generate non-taxable cash flow. The most common type of Permanent Insurance I've seen used on this basis is referred to as Universal Life. Normally, if you withdraw funds from the cash surrender value of your Universal Life policy it will attract some tax. However, there's no income tax on borrowed money.

The thought is that the policy is assigned to the bank as security for the funds you have borrowed. When you die, the benefits are paid to the bank. The bank then uses the proceeds to pay off any outstanding loans, plus accumulated interest. There's no tax on life insurance benefits. The balance of the benefits are then paid to your estate or heirs. This is a great concept in theory, and I've analyzed many Universal Life proposals for my clients. Unfortunately, when you cut through all the fancy sales material there are very few that I'm prepared to recommend.

One common problem is with the assumptions used to illustrate the potential advantages of the policy. In my experience, they're often not appropriate, and the illustrations are often confusing. So before proceeding with such a strategy, have it analyzed by a financial member of your transition advisory team who is familiar with these types of policies – someone who has no connection with the agent selling the insurance. In particular, make sure the analysis is done on a comparative basis. There are other assets that can compound on a tax-free basis. For example, compare it to putting the money into an investment like an Exchange Traded Fund or into certain types of mutual funds that can be tax-efficient.

There are a number of concerns with the leveraging strategy, whether you're borrowing against an insurance policy or a non-registered asset. If you're considering such a strategy, be sure to explore both the pros and cons of the equation.

A special need may exist

An example of a special need might be if you have a special child, who, after you're gone won't be able to provide for themselves financially. In this case, I recommend you talk to your lawyer or estate planner about the potential benefits of a permanent life insurance contract in combination with a "Henson Trust" (in Ontario, a trust worded so that as a child with disabilities is deemed not to have personally received the inheritance). Depending on the circumstances, it may be possible to leave the insurance policy to such a trust without affecting your child's right to certain government benefits.

You want to leave a specific amount to your heirs, a charity, a religious affiliation, or for some other special purpose.

This is an individual choice, for the most part. If you're interested in leaving funds to a charity or religious affiliation through an insurance policy of this type, there are some specialized tax benefits you may want to check into.

Disability Insurance

Disability insurance is very expensive, so it's important to make sure that you have the right amount of coverage for your unique circumstances. Generally, insurance companies will cover you to a maximum of 60 to 70% of your pre-tax income, so you'll have to decide what needs you want to cover with this insurance. Do you want to insure your income or do you want to insure your lifestyle and obligations? One may be much higher than the other.

It's my heartfelt view that you'll get the most value for the money you spend on disability coverage by matching it to the need you can't afford to underwrite yourself. The following is the form of analysis I would use to determine my own optimum disability insurance level.

Disability Insurance Needs Analysis

Add:

i.   An estimate of your annual personal lifestyle costs
ii. All payment obligations
iii. Savings needs for the children's education
iv. Savings needs for retirement

Deduct

i.   Spouse's salary if he/she will continue to work (note that if you're in solo practice and your spouse is employed in the practice, he/

she could be out of a job if you become disabled for any length of time)

ii. Investment income

iii. If you have the type of Office Overhead Insurance that will make payments on practice loans or have a practice contingency plan in place, you may want to deduct the cost of any debt service that arises out of the practice

Definitions of Disability

One of the most important things to understand about the policy you buy is the definition of "disability". The tighter the definition, the more expensive the coverage because there is a greater risk that the insurance company will have to pay out a benefit. For example, some policies may provide benefits if you're unable to perform the regular duties of your own occupation. Other policies state that you would only be considered disabled if you were unable to work at any job. The policy may also include a provision to provide benefits if you suffer a loss of income of, say 20% or more. Some policies have stringent definitions of disability or partial disability, while others are more broadly defined. It's important that you check the terms of the contract being proposed to you (or the one you currently have in place) to make sure you're comfortable with the definitions of disability.

Elimination Period

This is the length of time you must be disabled before you're eligible to collect the benefits. Typically you have the option of choosing 15 days, 30 days, 60 days, 90 days, or 180 days. The shorter the elimination period, the higher the premium. Remember that you'll get the greatest value from your insurance expenditures by insuring against risks that you can't afford to cover yourself. Most dentists don't need to spend the money to have a 15-day elimination period. You could be off that long with a bad flu virus.

Accounts receivable, cash reserves, hygiene and/or associate production, etc. will help to ease your loss of income from a short term absence from the office. I'd recommend you determine how long you could be away from work before it becomes a serious financial setback, and then structure your elimination period accordingly.

BARRY'S COACHING ADVICE

You may be able to save money by breaking up your policies with a variety of elimination periods.

The Benefit Period

Typically, the longer the benefit period, the higher the premium. It's worthwhile to carefully consider your needs to see if some will be eliminated over time. Examples here are loan payments that will amortize debt within a few years, and the education funding for your children.

Disability contracts and definitions are complex and vary from company to company. So make sure the person you're dealing with has in-depth knowledge of available product offerings. Where possible, try to get an idea about claims experience for a particular company before signing on the dotted line. I've heard horror stories from people who've had difficulty trying to collect their benefits when disabled, so be sure to ask the agent:

a) Are the benefits integrated with government programs?
b) What if I have an unknown pre-existing condition?
c) Does the policy have a maximum amount of benefits that can be paid out?

Office Overhead Insurance

Office Overhead Insurance is tax-deductible. While the premiums may seem expensive, there is some comfort in knowing that your government partner in Ottawa is prepared to, in effect, pay some of the expense. Therefore, it's prudent to obtain office overhead insurance to cover all of your fixed office expenses. To determine the amount of coverage needed, take the amount of your total expenses and deduct variable expenses such as supplies and laboratory costs. What you have left over is the amount of coverage you'll need. There are some people who believe that from this amount you should also deduct what your hygienists and associates are producing. This could be reasonable in a partnership or good cost-sharing arrangement.

For a solo practitioner, productivity of your hygiene department will typically decrease should you be off for an extended period. You may also have to factor in the cost of a locum. Associates are often graduates without the speed, patient communication skills and experience to easily fill your shoes.

Some Office Overhead Insurance programs offer a declining coverage option. As time goes on, they pay lower and lower percentages of your costs. For example, after 90 days benefits are reduced to 75% and so on. The lower premium cost with this type of insurance product can be quite appealing. In talking to dentists who have this type of coverage, the rationale invariably involves the idea of laying off staff. After all, if you're not working, what will the staff do anyway? I would recommend that you opt for the type of coverage that covers all of your fixed costs for at least one year or 18 months. Most dentists go back to their practices after a period of disability. While you're off, it's the staff's job to maintain, as much as possible, the goodwill of your patient base. Also, when you go back to work after a disability it's a great benefit to have trained staff familiar with your practice to support you. Trying to hire and train new people can be frustrating at the best of times. You'll have enough challenges returning to the office after a disability without having to worry about that, as well.

Key Person Insurance

Do you have someone in your practice who makes a critical contribution? Someone who would be very difficult to replace? If so, you may want to investigate getting some low cost term insurance on their life. This type of insurance is usually referred to as Key Person or Key Employee coverage. It's intended to protect the practice against the negative financial impact of the premature death of a highly valued employee who's integral to your success. Some business owners also insure such key employees for disability, but this is much more expensive.

Critical Illness Insurance

This is a relatively new insurance product with coverage similar in many ways to disability insurance. It's often employed in combination with disability coverage. Critical Illness Insurance could offer valuable coverage in the following situations:

- Providing cash to seek the best and most immediate treatment anywhere in the world
- Making an injection of cash available in case money must be spent on modifying your house and/or car to accommodate your affliction
- Paying off debt, particularly if you can't get enough disability coverage because of income limitations
- Supplementing your cash resources to make your last days more comfortable
- If you don't qualify for disability insurance for a reason that isn't medical, such as your earned income is not high enough

Critical Illness Insurance can be very expensive and it doesn't cover all illnesses, so be sure you understand what it does cover. A decision to buy this type of coverage is one you'll have to make, ideally with the help of your advisory team, after a careful analysis of the policy and your needs.

Long Term Care Insurance (LTCI)

LTCI is relatively new in Canada. It's intended to provide funding for care when you can no longer perform the usual activities of daily living. This is expensive coverage. Terms and definitions also vary from company to company. If you're considering such a policy, examine how they define "usual activities of daily living". Is it the insurance company who decides that you're eligible for such services, or is it some independent, unbiased third party? Also, in assessing whether or not you need this coverage, look at what it would cost today if you had to pay for the services covered under the contract directly.

A client who retired recently has more than sufficient capital to provide for an after-tax annual income, that is indexed, equal to what $120,000 would buy in today's dollars. In addition, they have a home and a cottage that are worth a significant amount of money and are free of debt. He and his wife were considering a long-term care policy. When we looked at what $120,000 after-tax would buy today in the way of such services, it became immediately clear that the client and his wife were self-insured. They didn't need to spend the money for this coverage. They could afford to underwrite the risk themselves.

General Insurance

Typically this includes your home, automobile, and practice. It could also include assets such as a boat or private aircraft. A detailed examination of each of these types of policies is beyond the scope of this book. However, let me emphasize that you should review this coverage regularly. It's not uncommon when I'm reviewing the affairs of a new client to find that their coverage is out of date.

Here are some questions you'll need to answer to guide your review of the policies:

1. Who is the insured?
2. What is the specific description of the asset or property that is insured?
3. Are the amounts of coverage still appropriate?
4. What risks are covered and are they appropriate in your circumstances?
5. Are there any exclusions?
6. Are the deductibles high enough? Keep in mind the rule about only insuring risks you can't afford to insure yourself. A good example of this is comprehensive insurance for your car. Many people pay extra money for a deductible that is quite low, for example

$50.00 or $100.00. Most of us can afford a loss of this sum.

7. Are there any coinsurance provisions? If you carry less coverage than the coinsurance requirement, a penalty may apply.

Umbrella Coverage

Umbrella Insurance is a form of liability insurance that fundamentally stands behind most of your other liability policies (except not malpractice). Anyone can find himself or herself in a situation where, for whatever reason, they face a significant liability. This insurance is inexpensive and in my view, the peace of mind makes the expenditure worth it. I once had a client sued for $5,000,000 because of an accident. His liability coverage only went up to $1,000,000. The good news is that after many years, the claim was finally settled for well under $1,000,000, so he was covered. But still, he and his family lived through years of uncertainty that could have been eliminated had he had Umbrella Coverage.

Malpractice Insurance

We live in an increasingly litigious world. To protect yourself, buy as much additional coverage as you possibly can, beyond what you get with your license.

Practice contingency plans

This doesn't apply to group practices. Typically group practice agreements provide for coverage should a member of the group either die or become disabled to the point where they can't return to practice.

If you're a solo practitioner, contingency planning for your practice is prudent. Ask yourself what would happen to your practice if you were to die prematurely or were disabled. Practices very often form a large part of a dental family's net worth. Goodwill is a perishable item. In the event of premature death, it's difficult enough for your grieving family without having to worry about quickly disposing of your practice. All the goodwill you've worked so hard to build up could be lost. Should you become disabled, it may be some time before you know whether or not you'll be able to return to practice. In the meantime, who's going to maintain your patient goodwill?

A practice contingency plan may consist of a simple set of policies and procedures within your office, or it could be a more elaborate program. For example, it could involve other solo practitioners in your area with whom you're willing to associate to deal with this common problem.

If you set up a simple plan within your office, I recommend you involve your staff in drafting the policies and procedures. After all, they are the ones who have to carry out the plan should something unexpected happen to you. The procedures would include instructions on how to reschedule patients, what to tell patients, and who to contact. Names and contact information for locums, practice brokers, and anyone else you may need to inform should be identified and kept up to date in the office policy manual.

Think about having the practice valued by a credible practice broker and have that valuation kept up to date. If the practice needs to be sold in a hurry, the existing valuation will be invaluable. Some practice brokers have programs whereby after the initial valuation, they update it every year for a nominal sum. Staff are generally in favour of this type of planning because it helps to assure them that they'll continue to have a job should some calamity affect the principal dentist where they're employed.

A self-protection group is another alternative in contingency planning for the practice. Solo practitioners all face the same problems in this area, so it's a good idea to establish an arrangement whereby everyone's practice is protected. While groups vary in size, a minimum of five practitioners is needed. Should one of the group either die or become disabled, there would be four practitioners left who would adjust their schedule so they could spend one day per week in the affected party's office.

In the case of death, there are a couple of ways to plan the contingency in a self-protection group...

OPTION ONE: have the surviving practitioners maintain the practice to facilitate the sale.

OPTION TWO: have the surviving practitioners buy the practice. Typically, insurance is put in place for the needed funding. This provides the deceased's family with ready cash and leaves the survivors free to dispose of the practice as they see fit, without the time constraints.

On the disability of one of the members of the group, the other parties would once again adjust their schedules so that they were able to maintain the disabled dentist's practice. Typically there's a time limit established, such as one year. At that point, it's expected that the disabled dentist will either return to work or the practice would be sold.

In all cases where members of the group are required to adjust their schedules to spend time at another party's practice, fair compensation should be paid. This may be an associate fee agreed upon when the group is set up, and it may or may not involve hygiene revenue. Each party will need to feel comfortable that they can trust the others to act in their best interests and not solicit either staff or patients.

Starting a group

If you're interested in starting such a group, begin by getting together with colleagues you trust and with whom you share common practice philosophies. Provided everyone is in agreement, you should document your understanding in a legal agreement. I'm not suggesting an agreement for the purposes of enforcement. Rather, it should be considered a communications document. It may be in place for a long time before it's needed (ideally, it will never be needed). Having a well-defined agreement allows members to remind themselves of the terms agreed upon.

Written (and signed) Practice Agreements

Far too many practices don't have good written agreements in place to properly define the complex relationships within their offices. Incidentally, you'll notice in the heading the words in brackets "and signed". This is another problem with agreements. Several times each year, I have the experience of working with a group practice situation only to find on reviewing their arrangements that the principals didn't sign their agreements. They went to the trouble of having them drawn up by a lawyer. They even refer to them from time to time. But they're not signed!

It's critical that you have well thought out agreements in place for the running of your practice, planning for contingencies, and management of your practice's value. This is particularly true if and when you're contemplating a transition. When dentists don't have such important documentation in place, it's usually because:

- They're very trusting and still believe in the concept of a "handshake"
- They're concerned about the potential legal expense
- Not understanding the complexities, they try to do it themselves
- They find the negotiation process preceding an agreement uncomfortable
- There are other priorities so they just never get around to it
- The parties know each other and consider themselves friends

To be candid, this lack of documentation is one of the reasons that many cost-sharing, associate, or partnerships don't work out. Practice agreements are best viewed as communication documents. Most people think that the primary purpose of an agreement is to have something to fall back on in the event of a dispute. I'd like to suggest that a well thought out agreement actually helps to prevent such disputes.

Over the years of working with dentists and helping them facilitate their agreements, I've found that overwhelmingly the parties want to be *fair* to each other. What do I mean by *fair*? Here we arrive at the crux of the problem. Interpretation as to what is or isn't fair varies from individual to individual. Generally, practice relationships don't fail because of dishonesty. If someone is dishonest, they'll find a way to 'disappoint' you whether there's an agreement in place or not.

In fact, most practice relationships that fail do so because each party had unmet expectations. This is why I recommend you focus on the communication aspects of agreements. Having an in-depth discussion about the important issues prior to entering into a relationship, helps the parties reach acceptable compromises in advance. If during this process you find that you can't agree, then be positive. Congratulate yourself. The system worked. It's so much better to find out that you're not compatible before entering into a relationship. You'll save money and you'll avoid all the stress and frustration of either living with an uncomfortable situation or breaking up. Having seen the effects of bad practice relationship breakups, I can't stress enough the importance of this process.

There's another reason to think of good practice agreements as communication documents - they tend to be in place for a long time. Over time, as everyone knows, memory fades, and interpretation can become distorted. If dealing with a contentious issue in the future, you'll always have the ability to refer back to your original understanding. Knowing you can always take the agreement out of the file, blow off the dust and see clearly what all parties intended gives you a method of dealing with disagreements before they become serious disputes.

BARRY'S COACHING ADVICE

Have a lawyer translate what you and your colleagues have agreed to into a functional legal agreement. When it comes to drafting agreements, deal with someone who is familiar with the practice of dentistry. Don't just accept the agreement that the lawyer proposes. Read it to make sure it expresses what you want. Each party to an agreement should have their own legal representation. Finally, if there's anything you don't understand, question it.

Wills and Powers of Attorney

I can't recall ever meeting a dentist who didn't understand that they needed a will or a power of attorney. Unfortunately, they didn't always have them in place or kept current. Once you do get them in place, make sure that your wills and powers of attorney are reviewed regularly and are always up to date. From a risk management perspective, this is as basic as telling your patients to brush regularly.

In summary

There's a lot about risk management that can be described as basic common sense. It's about recognizing that we don't always have control over the circumstances that befall us. But we do have control over how we handle them, and more importantly, how we prepare for them. With a little forethought, you can secure your potential for financial security and success against a variety of contingencies.

IN SUMMARY

Having read through the material in this book, you now have a comprehensive overview of what's involved in a successful transition. My hope is that this book becomes a valuable resource for you to turn to throughout your transition process. No doubt you'll find it helpful to re-read specific chapters or sections before making key decisions.

Now that you know about the process involved in a transition, there's one important thing you need to do: make it happen. This is where Attitude is Everything. I know from my experience as a financial planner working with dentists, that many of them at first feel discouraged about money management – and their transition prospects in general. Questions I often hear include:

- Where is the money for retirement savings supposed to come from?
- How can people plan the future when it's difficult enough to control the present?
- How much money will I need anyway?
- Will my RRSPs be enough?
- With my busy schedule, where can I find the time to plan and manage a successful transition?

Unfortunately, there's no end to questions of this nature, and if you can't answer them it can be very discouraging. However, I want you to know that I understand your concerns. Most importantly, I know that it's possible for you to take control and plan for a positive transition. After all, that's why I wrote this book, to help you along the road to the future you want and deserve.

The power of positive thinking

Much has been written about the power of positive thinking. You've probably heard about the importance of "vision" to outstanding athletes and successful corporations. Vision, by its nature, includes a positive outlook that the goal of either the individual or the group can be accomplished. What's important is the belief that success is possible.

When you think back, it's likely that you used positive thinking while getting through dental school. You would have had a vision of being a dentist as a pre-requisite, before embarking on the course of study that would lead to graduation. That vision was possible because there was a tried and true curriculum and a process that led you towards your objective. That doesn't mean it was easy. Becoming a dentist takes a lot of hard work. The point is you could entertain the vision of becoming a dentist because you knew it was possible. Others had done it before you and there was a road map to follow.

But where is the road map for dentists when it comes to financial and transition planning? That's another question that I've heard asked many times. In truth, it's no wonder there's so much confusion and uncertainty surrounding transition planning. In dental school they taught you how to be a good dentist. From that point on, there's been little or no training to guide you on how to go about the many business and financial activities to crown your professional career with a successful transition.

I have had the pleasure of working with dentists for over 20 years. This book is a culmination of that experience. It's not a theoretical treatise. It's a tried and true formula based on what I've seen work time and time again. Taking a proactive approach to your transition planning works. No matter what your circumstances, you'll always be better off, barring unforeseen calamities, taking the lead in your transition as outlined and encouraged in this book. I can't communicate this strongly enough. It's possible for almost every dentist to plan for a successful transition if they choose to do so. In fact, it's not only possible but it's your best hope for controlling the outcome.

BARRY'S COACHING ADVICE

Develop a "Positive Financial Attitude" (PFA).

With a PFA and the processes described in this book, it's possible for you to plan a successful transition. Just remember: Successful transitions happen by design.

In fact, let me take a moment to quickly recap the key processes covered in this book …

1. Put in place a transition advisory team.

Depending on your individual needs, knowledge base, time, etc., your team should consist of an accountant, lawyer, qualified financial planner and/or investment advisor (if they aren't one and the same), practice valuator, practice broker, perhaps a life planner, and any others you feel may be helpful. Remember, you can't do it all yourself. Even if you have the time it's unlikely you will have the necessary specialized training and experience. Some of the members of your team will be more active at certain times than others. It will be your job to make sure that they share information when it's required, as well as act in a coordinated manner and keep focused on your needs and objectives.

2. Establish well-defined, reasonable goals.

Have a member of your advisory team quantify them in financial terms so that they can be used as beacons to guide your journey towards transition. Be sure you understand and agree with the assumptions being used in these calculations.

3. Determine as accurately as possible where you are today in a financial sense.

I call this establishing your Current Position. It's your starting point for transition planning and the financial members of your team should be involved at this time. You may want to re-read chapters 2 and 3 to make sure you understand how to instruct these members of your advisory team and what to expect from them.

4. **Work with your transition advisory team to establish appropriate strategies.**

There are four strategy chapters in this book. One deals with introducing the topic and determining which of the following three chapters apply to you. Depending on your Current Position, one of these three remaining chapters on strategy should be appropriate for your circumstances. These strategies include making sure you're taking advantage of appropriate tax planning opportunities, some of which are discussed in this book. As well, your plan may include investment strategies designed to maintain the integrity of your capital, and these can be reviewed again in Chapter 9.

5. **Make sure your Risk Management is in order.**

6. **Monitor your progress and update your plan at least once annually.**

There's so much good news on the horizon

People are now living longer than ever before, and they also have an expectation of being healthy for a longer period than in previous generations. In a recent study done in the US, it was estimated that about 50% of all baby boomers will reach the age of 85. Hallmark estimates they sold over 80,000 100th birthday cards in a recent year. That's incredible. At the same time, there's a hidden message here. You could be retired longer than you practiced. If you're going to enjoy a financially comfortable retirement, your chances will be vastly improved by proactive transition planning. Procrastination is a major roadblock when it comes to transition planning, but you simply must take action. You can read all the books, listen to as many lectures as you can, and/or get additional training if you want. At the end of the day it will be a waste if you don't take action. It's up to you!

When is the best time to start planning your transition?

The answer to that is easy. When you graduate. Now to be candid, I have never met anyone who had this kind of foresight. I certainly didn't. So let me ask you another question. When is the next best time to start planning your transition? Once again this question is easy to answer. It's now!

On behalf of myself and my son, Mark McNulty, who also works as a financial planner with dental practitioners, I wish you and your family every success with your transition.

ISBN 141203563-5